Praise for *Leading Inclusion*

"If you are an executive who intends to build an inclusive organization but doesn't know where to start, *Leading Inclusion* will be uniquely helpful. Gena Cox uses an uncommon blend of storytelling, psychological science, and leadership insights to show how to lead inclusion for your company."

DORIE CLARK, *Wall Street Journal*–bestselling author, *The Long Game*; executive education faculty, Duke University's Fuqua School of Business

"This book stops you in your tracks and inspires you to be better. *Leading Inclusion* is an incredibly compelling and well-grounded call to leaders to lead inclusively."

DR. STEVEN ROGELBERG, Chancellor's Professor, organizational psychology, UNC Charlotte; past president, SIOP; bestselling author, *The Surprising Science of Meetings*

"In this ideas-packed and humane book, Gena Cox explains how we can overcome feeble excuses and cultural ignorance and take the bold steps required to change our workplace reality, one employee at a time."

DES DEARLOVE, cofounder, Thinkers50

"Implementing Gena Cox's well-researched practices and internalizing the deeply personal perspectives in *Leading Inclusion* will set your business up for success."

DR. TIFFANY JANA, CEO and founder, TMI Portfolio; award-winning coauthor, *Subtle Acts of Exclusion*

"Gena Cox's unique voice as a Black woman and organizational psychologist powers *Leading Inclusion* to reposition DEI as an executive leadership and corporate governance imperative."

DEEPA PURUSHOTHAMAN, cofounder, nFormation; author, *The First, the Few, the Only*

"Painstakingly researched yet practical, and nuanced yet digestible, *Leading Inclusion* is a must-read for every leader eager to build a culture of respect, equity, inclusion, and belonging."

GORICK NG, *Wall Street Journal*-bestselling author, *The Unspoken Rules*

"Gena Cox's timely call to action is a clear road map for any leader to enhance the inclusion experience of their organization."

DR. GRACE LORDAN, associate professor, behavioral science, and founding director, The Inclusion Initiative, London School of Economics; author, *Think Big*

"Gena Cox argues that DEI outcomes will change only when top-level leaders take action, and her powerful stories and insights show executives the way."

DR. THOMAS A. KOLDITZ, brigadier general, US Army (ret); director, Doerr Institute for New Leaders, Rice University

"A no-nonsense approach for conversations, learnings, and policy development to improve inclusion."

TONYA JACKSON, board director; SVP, Chief Product Delivery Officer, Lexmark

"A clear, doable playbook for top leaders to live up to their organization's promises on DEI. Gena Cox sets out smart and commonsense steps every leader should take."

KEN BANTA, founder and principal, The Vanguard Network

"A timeless arsenal of approaches that clarifies why we're not progressing as we should on inclusion and offers guidance for speeding up the process. It will open your eyes and heart."
RON CARUCCI, cofounder and managing partner, Navalent; bestselling author, *To Be Honest*

"This must-read book confirms that the inclusion journey does not have a finish line. Instead, it requires the C-suite's endless pursuit of creating and sustaining cultures that truly value the lived experience, particularly for people of color."
RHONDA S. BRANDON, MSOD, CHRO and SVP, Duke Health

"Gena Cox goes beyond standard DEI practices by explaining how top leaders can build an inclusive organization by using sound leadership practices that support and value each employee."
DR. PAUL E. SPECTOR, professor, business and organizational psychology, University of South Florida; author, *Job Satisfaction*

"A fascinating book that challenges organizational leaders to act and advance DEI. A great resource for MBA students."
DR. LEON C. PRIETO, professor, management, Clayton State University; coauthor, *African American Management History*

"*Leading Inclusion* will help you shift from inclusion intention to action. Gena Cox shares her lived experience as a Black woman executive navigating vastly differing corporate cultures. Highly recommended."
ELLEN TAAFFE, clinical professor, management and organizations, Kellogg School of Management; board director; former Fortune 50 executive

"*Leading Inclusion* is a must-read for all leaders who want to build a supportive, sustainable, and authentically inclusive organizational culture."

TRICIA MONTALVO TIMM, board director; DEI leader; author, *Embrace the Power of You*

"People of color are begging for the world of work to be reimagined. *Leading Inclusion* is our bold blueprint."

RHA GODDESS, founder and CEO, Move the Crowd; cofounder, nFormation; author, *The Calling*

"*Leading Inclusion* provides the outline for leaders who seek to win the war on talent through transformative and meaningful action."

AMII BARNARD-BAHN, JD, C-suite consultant; speaker; author, *The PI Guidebook*

"With plain talk, real-life examples, and thought-provoking questions, *Leading Inclusion* is a book of wisdom about how to be an extraordinary leader."

YOUNG MI PARK, board treasurer and secretary, American Marketing Association New York; lecturer, Rutgers Business School and Columbia University

"*Leading Inclusion* isn't just a book about diversity, equity, and inclusion; it's a book about effective and inclusive leadership."

CHARLENE A. WHEELESS, speaker; executive coach; author, *You Are Enough!*

"*Leading Inclusion* is a must-read for business leaders who want to do more than 'check the DEI box.'"

AJ HARPER, author, *Write a Must-Read*

LEADING
INCLUSION

DRIVE CHANGE YOUR EMPLOYEES CAN SEE AND FEEL

GENA COX, PhD

LEADING INCLUSION

PAGE TWO

Cataloguing in publication information is available from Library and Archives Canada.
ISBN 978-1-77458-179-7 (hardcover)
ISBN 978-1-77458-180-3 (ebook)
ISBN 978-1-77458-278-7 (audiobook)

Page Two
pagetwo.com

Edited by Kendra Ward
Copyedited by Jenny Govier
Proofread by Alison Strobel
Jacket design by Peter Cocking
Interior design by Fiona Lee
Indexed by Stephen Ullstrom
Printed and bound in Canada by Friesens
Distributed in Canada by Raincoast Books
Distributed in the US and internationally by Macmillan

22 23 24 25 26   5 4 3 2 1

leadinginclusion.com

To my daughter, Marin.
You power my dream that women like us can
thrive in a future, better workplace.

Contents

· · · · · · · · · · · · · · ·

Introduction

"HIRE MORE people of color. Check! Provide implicit bias training for all employees in the company. Check! Hire a Chief Diversity Officer. Check! I've done all the things my advisors recommended, yet our employee survey results are tanking, and we are losing many of our 'diversity' hires almost as quickly as we can hire them. I don't have more time to allocate this diversity, equity, and inclusion work, but my board wants better results. Help!"

Carol, the energetic, innovative, and socially aware technology leader who said this to me, is a product innovation and growth strategy wunderkind. Her leadership superpowers have pushed her company onto many "fastest-growing" lists; she is a leader to admire. And yet, she feels insecure about meeting stakeholders' diversity, equity, and inclusion (DE&I) expectations. Despite her best intentions, her DE&I efforts are criticized and underappreciated, and her organization has very little progress to show for their year of action in this area. Carol is unsure what to do next.

I regularly hear similar frustrations from other well-intentioned corporate leaders who don't understand *why* their DE&I efforts are missing the mark. Yet, when I analyze the details, I often find that they did not diagnose their company's unique DE&I challenges before implementing the flavor-of-the-month DE&I solution. Or, they have superimposed DE&I recruiting and training solutions upon an unhealthy organizational culture in which manager and leader behavior is not inclusive. A small circle of employees may still be getting the prized promotions, and the board and C-suite may still lack diversity. Sometimes, executives' actions don't land because they lack an overall strategy for building an inclusive organization. And I regularly see executives approach this work from a safe distance, having lobbed the ball to the "DE&I experts," apparently hoping not to get their hands dirty if things don't work out as planned. No wonder employees of color are miserable and no real DE&I progress occurs!

The most accurate way to gauge DE&I progress is to understand the reactions of the stakeholders who matter the most: employees. Not just employees of color—all employees. If employees can't see and feel meaningful DE&I outcomes, they will not believe their leaders are building an inclusive organization. They will leave, and it will be hard to attract other employees of color. Effective inclusion leadership needs to start at the top of the organization. All employees will benefit: employees of color, women, men, LGBTQ+, the neuro- and physio-diverse, immigrants, those who struggle to speak English... everyone.

On Monday, May 25, 2020, a police officer in Minneapolis, Minnesota, knelt on George Floyd's neck for nine minutes and twenty-nine seconds, killing him. Television stations and internet channels continuously streamed videos of this ultimate act of inhumanity. Just two months earlier, police officers had fired shots into Breonna Taylor's apartment, killing her.

I watched corporate executives and board directors paying attention to these unjust events, but their responses often betrayed their unfamiliarity and discomfort with the work. Employees (of all races), customers, and investors were asking CEOs, "Do any of the concerns revealed in the public social justice conversations occur in your organization?" and "What are you doing to be part of the solution?" Executives could no longer avoid the issue. The calls for justice were *inside* the corporate walls, and stakeholders would not allow leaders to push these concerns back out.

I decided to use my unique training and experience as a PhD organizational psychologist, executive coach, Black woman, mother, and immigrant to help business leaders address this persistent inclusion challenge in America's workplaces.

This book is the result of that decision. I wrote it to show leaders like you how to lead an inclusive organization, by setting a vision for diversity and inclusion and cascading it into the organization. The goal is to lead in a way that employees can see and feel the difference in their day-to-day work experiences. In this book I focus on the inclusion experiences of people of color, primarily Black people, in US workplaces. Nevertheless, the insights can enhance the work environment for *any* employee, regardless of their natural human variation.

Race and ethnicity classifications vary significantly across the globe, as do the histories and social forces influencing the human experience. However, race-based mistreatment is the most commonly reported form of workplace discrimination in the US, and racial equality is still elusive in broader society. Employees of color, particularly Black employees, continue to face occupational segregation that pushes them to the bottom of the workplace hierarchy.

Although racial diversity is increasing in the US, segregation, especially in big cities, was worse in 2019 than in 1990,
and most Americans still live segregated lives. Our neighborhoods and churches are often more segregated than our
workplaces. Moreover, racial and socioeconomic segregation
seem to have hardened to the point that Americans have little
contact with and do not understand one another across race
and "class." As a result, we are more likely to interact with
people of a different race at work than in most other social
situations.

Let's take advantage of this relative "togetherness" that
exists in the workplace. In the past, when racial justice issues
have reached the headlines, some business leaders have done
nothing or as little as possible. After decades of "as-little-
as-possible" action, hiring rates have improved little for people of color, and fewer than expected people of color hold
executive leadership roles in corporate America today.

This time can be different.

We likely have some things in common, since you are
reading this book. We are looking for solutions to the racially
based discomfort, discontent, and disappointment that per-
vades many employees' experiences. What if workplaces
could become havens of inclusion where employees work
well together, despite their human variations? And what if
those same employees spread that goodwill into the broader
society? Maybe inclusion at work could translate into inclusion in schools, playgrounds, churches, and communities.
Perhaps we could change America, one employee at a time.
But where would we begin?

Until May 2020, I had been satisfied using my organizational psychology expertise to advise global corporate
executives on building engaging work cultures. My clients
wanted to drive innovation and productivity to meet the

demands of a changing world, and they demanded "data-based" recommendations. However, I knew that if we could toss aside the analyses for a minute and engage in straight talk, leaders' actions might be more impactful. The real deal is that most of the employee engagement and employee experience problems organizations faced came down to one thing: weak manager capability and poor manager behavior. And often, employees of color were less engaged than other employees because their managers treated them differently than others they led.

So, in response to the angst I was experiencing after George Floyd's and Breonna Taylor's deaths, I pivoted to guiding leaders to strategic solutions to persistent race-based disparities in corporate employee experiences. For the first time, I believed leaders and other stakeholders were ready to engage in this conversation—and I was ready to give them some compelling insights to ponder. I started by pulling in insights from psychological science, other corporate leaders, DE&I researchers and practitioners, and my own experience in corporate America. Race-based disparities in organizations can only be solved if executive leadership drives the action, so I designed a strategic framework to help leaders act.

You are a well-intentioned corporate leader navigating a new landscape that requires a more in-depth understanding of DE&I issues. This book, a map for that journey, helps you reframe your thoughts so you can lead the other leaders in your organization (including a Chief Diversity Officer or Chief Human Resources Officer, if you have one). You will learn which key questions you should ask, the constituents you must address, and the actions you must take to be successful in your quest to build an inclusive organization.

The guidance in this book is organized into four sections.

Part One, Skin in the Game, explores the historical facts that created and reinforced many of the race-based social disparities we see in corporate life today.

Parts Two, Three, and Four lay out my three-step **Inclusion MBA** framework for leader-driven corporate inclusion: **Mindset, Boldness, and Action.**

Part Two, the Mindset section, frames the experience of a top leader regarding diversity and inclusion issues within the realities of organizational life. First, you need to explore what you believe about these issues. Your beliefs influence your decisions and actions, and sometimes that influence is outside your consciousness. Nevertheless, those around you—other leaders and employees at every level—will notice those actions. It is best that you, your executive team, and your board explore your beliefs before developing or implementing an inclusion strategy.

Part Three, the Boldness section, will help you get an accurate picture of the current experience of *all* your employees and the confidence to make sometimes unpopular decisions to address race-based disparities. This section reminds you to set clear expectations in your communications to the stakeholders you want to bring along on your inclusion journey, including direct reports, organization leaders and managers, employees, and board directors. They must all be on board.

Part Four, the Action section, provides science- and experience-based insights to help you identify actions that might work for your organization. By the end of Part Four, you should know what you will do next, depending on where you are in your journey.

I offer the guidance in this book from the perspective of my twenty-five-plus years' experience advising corporate executives as an organizational psychologist and executive coach. I also use the frame of my personal experience as a Black woman in corporate America. As with most Black Americans, my professional identity has never superseded my racial identity. While I sometimes get extra points for being an organizational psychologist, I simultaneously deal with almost-daily race-based slights. I have lived many of the challenges discussed in this book. I know what it feels like to be gaslighted (when a leader, to assert their power and keep you hooked and hopeful, denies their actions that you have seen or experienced). I know what it feels like to be bread-crumbed (when a leader gives you small bits of communication and encouragement that never lead to the desired outcome, like a promotion or pay raise, for example). And I have been excluded in many of the ways authors Drs. Tiffany Jana and Michael Baran describe in their book *Subtle Acts of Exclusion* (SAE): through nuanced words and actions driven by conscious and unconscious bias. The SAEs I have experienced include conveniently "missed" invitations to networking and other career-building opportunities, being overlooked for promotions despite my ample qualifications, and having colleagues ignore my verbalized ideas as if I were invisible. Some of the other peculiar exclusions and avoidances you will read about in this book might surprise you. But, since I have dealt with and helped others deal with these experiences, I know they are commonplace in corporate life.

Although they have been discussed more frequently since May 2020, I realize that these experiences are neither universally experienced nor universally understood. And I recognize that you may not fully "get" the Black woman's experience nor understand yet why this perspective offers valuable insights for your leadership inclusion journey. However, I hope the stories, science, and experiences shared in this book will show you that Black employees' experiences are a uniquely informative microcosm of the overall employee experience. When Black employees have positive experiences at work, all other employees are also likely doing well too, because our experiences tend to be the least positive. Our experiences may reveal the hidden, bottom-of-the-barrel realities of the day-to-day employee experience in your organization, for all races. And of course, those revelations will point to the improvements you can lead.

In 1892, Black feminist scholar Anna Julia Cooper wrote that Black women suffer from "both a woman question and a race problem." Almost exactly one hundred years later, in 1989, Dr. Kimberlé Crenshaw, a Black woman, lawyer, and scholar, coined the term "intersectionality" to illuminate the complex social factors (including identity) that determine power and powerlessness. Unfortunately, the intersectional experience of Black women in American workplaces is uniquely fraught. On one hand, Black women can be hyper-visible, leading to us being stereotyped as "threatening." Yet on the other, as Lean In's research shows, we can also be invisible, leading to us receiving less career development support in corporate America than women of any other race or ethnic group. That double bind gets some attention in this book.

Over the years, I have read every piece of research regarding the experience of Black people in the workplace I could find. I learned that my own experiences of exclusion are not unique. If anything, I have been fortunate. My education, accent, and practiced poker face garnered me more grace and privilege than many others who look like me.

It would be easy for me to write a book from solely my Black woman's or industrial-organizational (I/O) psychologist's perspective. However, I also include the view of those on the other side of the corporate concrete ceiling: corporate executives. Between December 2020 and September 2021, I interviewed fourteen executive leaders (present and former Chief Executive Officers (CEOs) and Chief Human Resource Officers, and board directors). I asked them to share their goals, hopes, fears, questions, and advice about respect, equity, diversity, and inclusion (REDI)—the term I use instead of "diversity, equity, and inclusion" (DE&I). I will explain REDI in the coming pages. These leaders shared openly and were brutally honest. Some of them asked that these conversations be off the record, explaining that although they want to lead the REDI effort in their organizations, they had not yet done enough. Many said they were in the "listening and learning" phase and were not role models for other leaders. Some said they were afraid to talk openly about race in the workplace. Some leaders asked that their comments be incorporated into the book without attribution, because "race" is still a taboo topic in their worlds. These leaders voiced *questions and concerns* that I could address in the book, and I have provided answers from my research and experience and the research and experience of other psychology scholars, REDI practitioners, and executive coaches. **My extensive research about leading inclusion effectively is the basis for my conclusions and recommendations in this book. Rather than provide traditional in-text note callouts, I've provided detailed Notes (by page number) and Further Reading sections (by chapter) for those who want to use this book as an education or research tool.**

I want you to feel empowered to act not just to improve diversity but also to enhance feelings of inclusion for all who work in the companies you lead. This book is your partner as you work to make America better, one employee at a time.

The REDI
Outcomes Model

Respect
Equity
Diversity
Inclusion

PART ONE

SKIN IN THE GAME

. . . .

The Skin in the Game Precondition

*My respect, equity, diversity, and inclusion journey
starts with my willingness to listen.*

1

CEOs Can Change America, One Employee at a Time

Those who tell you "Do not put too much politics in your art" are not being honest. If you look very carefully you will see that they are the same people who are quite happy with the situation as it is... What they are saying is don't upset the system.
CHINUA ACHEBE, *Conversations with James Baldwin*

I SUSPECT YOU think your biggest diversity and inclusion challenge is hiring more people (of color or other human variation). But if you are struggling to establish a truly diverse and inclusive workplace, the key is actually defining behavior expectations for all leaders and employees in your organization.

On June 19, 1865, Union soldiers informed the last enslaved Africans in the US of their emancipation. Black Americans celebrate Juneteenth, on June 19, each year to commemorate this highly significant historical event. So, I stopped in my tracks when, in June 2020, I heard *several* CEOs say, "I didn't know anything about Juneteenth! I don't know what to say or do about Juneteenth! Should I celebrate it in my company or not? How *should* I celebrate it? Should I give employees the day off?" And so on.

That was my aha moment: CEOs and employees did not know how to respond, at work, when race-related issues surfaced.

But why not?

I agree with Satya Nadella, the CEO of Microsoft, that being a "learn-it-all" is better than being a "know-it-all." Still, in my more than twenty years of advising executive leaders, I have seldom heard an executive say they did not "know." This time was different. A pandemic was raging, social injustices were fomenting, and the mood in the country was darkening.

The uncertainty I was hearing in leaders' voices was a good sign; a sign of self-awareness and necessary vulnerability. For the first time, leaders were publicly acknowledging their unfamiliarity with the experiences of people of color in the US, and in their organizations. They realized that the same old rules of avoidance and silence would be insufficient for this new day.

Not Knowing about the Black Experience

According to the US Census, the overall US population is about 76 percent White and 13 percent Black. However, data from the US Bureau of Labor Statistics indicate that about 86 percent of chief executives in the US labor force are White and only about 6 percent are Black. It is, therefore, not surprising that a CEO might not know about Juneteenth. He (71 percent of US chief executives are men) would likely only know about Juneteenth if, while growing up, he regularly interacted with Black people. Or if he attended a school where the teachers were Black. Or if he was lucky enough to have been specifically taught "African American" history in school (unlikely, since even now, many US school boards exclude books from their curricula that cover this subject). And although Black History Month celebrations are commonplace, they tend to highlight the same well-known Black leaders each year, glossing over the ugly underbelly of slavery's impact that is more visible in the stories and lives of "ordinary" Black Americans. Black History Month is itself a sign of the problem. As actor Morgan Freeman noted, "I don't want a Black History Month. Black history is American history."

I didn't grow up in the US, but I "officially" became a "Black American" about a year after moving here. It happened the day someone called me the N-word; you never forget your first time! After that, I began to read voraciously about the Black experience in America because it would now be *my* experience. That study is how I learned about Juneteenth. However, it was not until 2020, forty years later, that I understood why this uniquely evocative commemoration of American history is not well known outside the Black American community.

Since I was now a Black American too, I needed to catch up on all the things I would now experience for which I had no precedent; I needed to know how to "be." I needed to understand why I should not walk alone at night in certain places, and the significance of the unfamiliarly negative reactions I experienced when I walked into a room. I needed to understand why my graduate school internship coordinator referred me to a clerical assistantship at a national burger chain rather than a research assistant role at the Naval Air Warfare Center Training Systems Division, as she did for my classmates. Indeed, I didn't want to study war, but surely she knew I could do better than the clerical job!

On my former island home, Barbados, people encouraged and celebrated me and told me regularly that I would excel. But, when I came to the US, it seemed as if a veil of low expectations dropped in front of me. Suddenly, I was being disregarded instead of encouraged. I was the same Gena, but the people around me only saw and responded to an avatar of "Black Woman." If society's mirror consistently reflected a distorted, fun-house version of me, was I still "Gena"?

These experiences engendered complex feelings, and I quickly became adept at handling them. And by "handling," I mean internalizing. I seldom spoke about the experiences or the emotions. Looking back, I should have found a more effective way of dealing with the racial trauma I was experiencing. But all paths to better seemed paved with high risk! I felt powerless to hold accountable those who perpetuated the racism. And while the powerful *might* have been able to help, they seemed uninterested in even talking about these issues, never mind taking action to solve them. So, I never spoke of my troubles at work, and leaders never noticed the problem.

I am not the only one. That pattern of ineffective avoidance and silence is one of the reasons why racism persists in the workplace. Racial discrimination and the resulting trauma are like a national medical mystery; the pain is real but the source is often not known or acknowledged. And yet, whether you experience it or not, racism exists in America, and the trauma it inflicts is omnipresent and very real for those on the receiving end. Healing from racism requires action and support, including from those who have not experienced it and don't understand it. Healing from racism requires people of color to change how we show up at work, but it also requires action from those who have the power to change workplaces. Healing from racism is difficult but necessary for all of us to be psychologically healthy!

REDI is a "respect-first" model because if leaders don't first ensure that underrepresented employees feel respected, none of the other outcomes will matter, nor will they be sustainable.

Social Segregation, Street by Street

I live in a lovely little town in Tampa Bay, Florida. I noticed many years ago that part of the town is somewhat cut off from the rest. That section has smaller homes, and some of the streets lack sidewalks. A seemingly required railroad track runs through the town, dividing one area of that smaller-house neighborhood from other larger-house sections. The topography is low and prone to settling water. One portion of the community is a large cul-de-sac for which there is only a single point of entry and egress. And then, there is a unique touch, which even most locals might overlook: many of the streets in the smaller-house neighborhood are named after trees (for example, Elm and Maple). Those tree-named streets are in the "Black" neighborhood. The street names inexplicably change when you cross the large road separating this smaller-house neighborhood from the larger houses.

Locals created that naming convention (also seen in many other Southern US towns) as a convenient line of demarcation between White streets and Black streets, so White people could avoid the "Black" neighborhood by avoiding the tree-named roads. It's an elegant solution to a hateful, inelegant problem!

Social segregation is such a well-oiled and pervasive tool that we don't notice it unless it negatively affects us. Many Americans have no friends of another race and, therefore, may not realize how much the quality and experiences of day-to-day life in America vary by race and ethnicity. But the fact is that many people of color experience racial harassment every day, often starting as early as grade school. Segregation powers misunderstanding, underestimation, and subordination of "others." Black Americans are among the "others," and this social segregation is a primary reason a CEO might not know about Juneteenth or the Black experience writ large.

If you don't have that connection, you might not know what Black employees experience every day in the company you lead. You might be unaware of the trauma and pain your Black employees carry. Or that some of that trauma is being exacted and exacerbated by managers within your company. Finally, you might not know that Black employees need *your* help to function with *ease rather than dread* in your organization.

Thinking more clearly about this issue blew my mind, but it also revealed how I could best contribute to the "struggle." I could take a cynical approach and say, "How come you don't know these things, Mr. CEO?" Or, I could use my knowledge and experience to share a more nuanced understanding of the Black American experience and how it affects our daily lives at work. I chose the second path. I want to inform your understanding of this unique leadership challenge and build your confidence about infusing inclusion into your business strategies, organizational culture, and leader behavior.

Caged Bird

My company gave employees a day off on June 19, 2020, and asked that we use the time to learn about the Black experience. The following week my colleagues recited their "epiphanies" much like one would describe a compelling piece of museum art. While my colleagues described their learning as "history," to me, these "ahas" sounded like the naive retelling of my own contemporary experience. I reached my limit when one young man related vivid details about a movie that depicted grotesque deaths on trees. I didn't need to know any more about lynching! The racial divide felt like a chasm that day.

At the time this scenario played out, I was a seasoned professional and a culture "expert" at the company. I had a PhD in organizational psychology and decades of experience that powered what our clients wanted to buy. However, I felt totally disconnected from my colleagues. Their "storytelling" made me feel they had just "discovered" Black people for the first time. But I, the Black person, felt like a caged bird in a system that was clearly not built with my emotional needs in mind. Plus, I had been there all along, hidden in plain sight!

The following Sunday, June 28, 2020, I felt fidgety. Twelve-year-old Keedron Bryant was singing a song of lamentation on the 2020 BET Awards show, "I Just Wanna Live." I wasn't looking forward to going to work the next day, and the video accompanying this young man's wailing just added to my pathos. I cried, for about twenty minutes. In that moment I realized I had to stop faking it.

So, I "came out as Black."

I acknowledged that for the decades I had been advising corporate leaders, very few of my clients understood how difficult it had been for me on days when I showed up with the painted-on smile. I had done such an effective job of pushing down my feelings of exclusion at work that I had become a numb hypocrite. I advised executives how to build engaging and satisfying work cultures, while simultaneously feeling invisible, undervalued, excluded, and dissatisfied in my own jobs!

Feeling Unprepared to
Deal With Racial Justice Issues

As a business leader, you are accustomed to setting a vision, defining a strategy, and releasing the full power of employees' efforts to execute that shared vision. You do that every day, with your product or service offering strategy, with your marketing and sales strategies. But you don't usually get deeply involved with REDI issues. Instead, you typically hand off these issues to your Chief Human Resources Officer (CHRO) or Chief Diversity Officer (CDO), getting involved only to provide funding or political approval of their initiatives. But unfortunately, that approach will not work in this "Future-Now" work world.

Much of the REDI work done in organizations for the past fifty-plus years, since the US Equal Employment Opportunity Commission (EEOC) was created, has had only minimal impact relative to money and time invested. This work is typically handled like a "check the box" obligation, focusing more on administrative procedures than enhancing employee experiences. Professionals responsible for managing REDI programs often have minimal clout and few resources. This reminds me of the Dutch boy who stuck his finger into a hole in a dyke to stop the water from entering his town. The villagers treated him like a hero the next day, but he almost froze overnight, waiting for someone to come up with a permanent solution to the leaky dyke. In that story, villagers eventually devised a solution, but REDI professionals seem to be perpetually stuck trying to plug the hole! They get little support for sustainable solutions and their contributions are not highly valued.

You may have underestimated the scope of the race-based disparities that play out in larger society and in your organization, too. These disparities result from a long history of slavery and a general intolerance for differences in the US. But, if you have never heard these facts discussed openly or if they have not been part of your education, you might be oblivious to the scale of the problem.

You might even believe your organization is already doing all it can or should to address REDI issues. Your CHRO and CDO have likely implemented actions meant to minimize disparities based on race, ethnicity, gender, LGBTQ+ status, disability, age, and other protected human variations. But, unfortunately, those actions likely have not had the desired impact, at least not from the perspective of those whose opinions matter most: employees!

Research shows that White job applicants receive 36 percent more callbacks than Black applicants and that hiring rates for Black Americans did not improve in the twenty-five years between 1990 and 2015. People of color, especially Black women, continue to be underrepresented in leadership roles and persistently report less positive day-to-day experiences at work than their colleagues of other races and ethnicities. Although highly represented in technology jobs, Asian Americans are the least likely to be promoted to leadership roles in those jobs.

Your stakeholders are popping up with questions about these issues because they want your company to be a place where all employees can thrive, and they want to be on the right side of history when the dust settles. As a leader, you must be informed about these issues—especially when they could be happening in your organization. And if you delegate the solutions, you must maintain oversight; *you* need to lead the conversation to ensure your organizational culture supports inclusion. So, let's take that journey together!

What to Do When Something Bad Happens

When leaders ask me what to say or do about calls for social justice, I know exactly how to direct them. "Race" has long been on some imaginary list of "The Top Five Things We Should Never Talk About at Work" (along with sex, money, politics, and religion)! I made up that list, but research shows that talk of race is taboo, especially for people from traditionally subordinated groups. Many people of color minimize their negative experiences at work simply by keeping silent, and although there are legal protections against workplace discrimination, most people do not use them—the risk is perceived to be too great. Mr. Floyd's death provided incontrovertible evidence our society had reached a new low point that required major change. Government leaders, business leaders, and Black people cannot deny it. That is how I frame my guidance to leaders; this is a new day.

In this new day, you *can* do things that will help with healing and forward movement.

You can start with my REDI 10/4 model, which suggests ten actions you can take to make a positive difference and four you should avoid. These are short-term tactics; ultimately, you need to build scalable solutions that will stand the test of time. We'll discuss more about the "how" in upcoming chapters.

REDI 10/4 Effective Actions

When a social justice and diversity and inclusion issue occurs, do this:

1 **Get out front.** You may think of it as an "HR issue" to delegate to your CHRO. Resist that temptation, especially

if you have not previously discussed race matters in your organization. As a CEO, C-suite executive, or board director, you must take the lead. Employees are waiting for you to soothe their anxieties and support them. They are also waiting for you to "own" the conversation. If you do anything less, you will lose credibility.

2 **Communicate with employees first.** Before you communicate with the press or other public media about the issue, communicate with your team.

3 **Communicate as soon as possible.** Employees may interpret a delay as a lack of concern, or worse, a lack of leadership courage.

4 **Acknowledge your feelings.** Share that you too have feelings about the situation and that your feelings likely mirror theirs. Their feelings are not alien. Empathize.

5 **Communicate with *all* employees.** All employees, regardless of their human variation, are likely to be aware of the issue. Individual opinions and levels of empathy may vary, but you should let *all* employees know that you recognize the significance of the moment. Don't address your communications just to the victim's identity group.

6 **Provide quick, sensible support.** Do not wait to provide support, which could include mental health or financial support, and so on. But talk to your employees to decide on the fine-grained actions that may be necessary. Let your employees tell you what they need.

7 **Give employees a forum.** Provide mechanisms for employees to express their feelings and to tell you and their managers what they need. Focus groups, town halls, and

other group forums work well for this purpose. Make it easy for employees to individually connect with you, their manager, and human resources leaders.

8 **Develop a "crawl-walk-run" communication/connection strategy.** So that employees don't feel cornered and have time to think about what they want to say, use a gradual yet consistent approach, especially if this is the first time employees have been given "permission" to talk about race at work.

9 **Listen and analyze.** You may be champing at the bit and your first instinct might be to implement implicit bias training, to educate about diversity, and to make enterprise-wide proclamations. Avoid this approach. After your initial communications and support, look at data that can inform your subsequent actions. That data will come primarily from the listening sessions, focus groups, surveys, and your human resources information system. Your employees will respond more positively if your actions are driven by data and insights that align with their experiences. And you will be more confident and less reluctant to make the necessary bold moves.

10 **Use employee surveys to get fine-grained data.** Employee opinion surveys allow employees to express their opinions anonymously. The other significant advantage is that they allow you to slice the data in meaningful ways for your organization (for example, by business unit or division).

REDI 10/4 No-Nos

When employees are coping with social justice and diversity and inclusion issues:

1 **Do not talk only to the employees of the group directly affected.** It may be tempting to talk only to the Black people or the Asian American people, and so on, in your organization. That approach further "otherizes" those employees. Some people who look like the victims may not want to talk about the issue at all. Additionally, employees *not* from that group will have been impacted too and will also need support. Assume that all employees, not just those who look like the victims, want to be part of the solution.

2 **Do not assume that employees from the targeted group will share their experiences unprompted.** These are highly emotional experiences. Employees may need time to process their feelings and to deal with the recurring trauma. Employees may also worry about job security and about being labeled as troublemakers if they express their true feelings. Give them space to talk, but let them decide when the time is right.

3 **Do not ask the most senior person from the targeted group to be the company's spokesperson for the issue.** The CEO should be the first person to speak to employees and anyone else on behalf of the organization, even if the most senior person from the targeted group chooses to lead employee-focused solutions. The well-worn tactic of having the most senior person of the targeted group speak first telegraphs that this is an issue for "them" and does not concern the entire organization. And although that

leader may want to help, they will need space to process their own emotions.

4 **Do not ask the marketing department to highlight the targeted group in ways that seem performative or inauthentic.** If you haven't previously included the target group in your advertising or collateral materials (for example, your website), you should certainly do so. However, an abrupt 180-degree turn in which you put the target group front and center in all visuals will likely generate a skeptical response from employees and other stakeholders. Better to acknowledge the deficiency and then ask marketing to ensure that all future marketing materials are inclusive, as they should have been all along.

ESSENTIAL DEFINITIONS

Some of the terms I use in this book may be unfamiliar, so before we go too far, I'd like to take a few minutes to align on the language.

REDI: This stands for respect, equity, diversity, and inclusion. I use this acronym in place of D&I (diversity and inclusion) or DE&I (diversity, equity, and inclusion). REDI is a "respect-first" model because if leaders don't first ensure that underrepresented employees feel respected, none of the other outcomes (equity, diversity, inclusion) will matter, nor will they be sustainable.

Respect: My definition of "respect" is this: the degree to which you acknowledge another human and treat them the way you would want to be treated, regardless of their station in life. Aretha Franklin sang about "R-E-S-P-E-C-T" because respect is the

Humans vary,
and human
variation
is normal.

word Black Americans use to express the emotion of being accepted. The term "belonging" is similar but less evocative and requires a longer incubation period. Respect must be immediate and automatic, like justice. Black people want to be respected and given the benefit of the doubt, unless there is some logical reason we should be disrespected. Therefore "respect" is first in the REDI acronym: it is the primary outcome that Black people seek in corporate spaces.

Equity: The E in REDI stands for "equity." It is about "each of us getting what we need to survive or succeed—access to opportunity, networks, resources, and supports—based on where we are and where we want to go." Equity and equality are not the same. Equity aims to provide the support each person (or group) needs to get to a valued outcome. Equality is about establishing processes to ensure that all people (or groups) get *the same* outcome. In some situations, getting to the same outcome does not make sense.

Let's say an organization analyzed its talent mobility data and identified a systematic pattern where one group of employees (for example, women) moved into its executive jobs less often than men. Through an equity lens, an appropriate response would include talking directly to both men and women to determine if they value the same or different things, and how those values affected their career choices. The women might be intentionally avoiding the traditional career paths, because those roles don't support their *life* expectations! In that case, it would be better to redesign new, equally well-regarded career paths so that there are multiple points of entry to executive roles. Success might mean that the women get executive roles via different paths than the men.

Examined from an equality lens, one might automatically steer the women toward the "traditional" path, thinking that success means having equal proportions of men and women in those roles. Some women might take the roles because that is the only route to the career outcomes they seek, even if at odds with their personal desires or obligations. And they might be miserable the entire time! As with many talent processes, an equality-based solution might work for the company but be less effective than an equity solution.

Diversity and inclusion: The words "diversity" and "inclusion" often appear as twins because neither term, independently, encompasses the breadth of the challenge each seeks to define. Diversity is about the degree to which your workforce reflects the demographic characteristics of the available labor force. Inclusion is focused on organizational systems and processes that factor in social support for all employees, including traditionally subordinated groups. I like to say that diversity is about counting the numbers of people of color (or other human variation), while inclusion is about whether those people feel respected, seen, heard, and empowered, like all other employees. The two elements are complementary.

Race: This term is a social construct, not a biological fact. I use the definition from the National Human Genome Research Institute: "Race is a fluid concept used to group people according to various factors including ancestral background and social identity… [or] people that share a set of visible characteristics, such as skin color and facial features." The 2020 US Census identified the following race categories: White; Black or African

American; American Indian or Alaska Native; Asian; and Native Hawaiian or Other Pacific Islander. According to the US Census, "Hispanic/Latino" is an ethnicity, not a race.

Ethnicity: I use the definition from the American Psychological Association: "Ethnicity refers to shared cultural characteristics such as language, ancestry, practices, and beliefs." The Hispanic/Latino ethnic group comprises people from a variety of races.

Traditionally underrepresented or subordinated groups: I use these terms in place of "minority" because "minority" can be equated with being "less than," while "underrepresented" or "subordinated" gets to the central concern. Since this book is focused on race and ethnicity, I include Black/African Americans, Hispanic/Latinos, Asian Americans and Pacific Islanders (AAPI), and Native Americans in this category. Note, however, that "Native Americans" prefer to be called by their specific tribal affiliations. It is best to ask individuals how they prefer to be addressed, regardless of race or ethnicity.

"Black" or "African-American"? In this book, I use the term "Black" to describe people who might variously be identified as "Black," "African American," "of African descent," or in other ways. None of these terms is universally acceptable to the people they are meant to identify. I have chosen "Black" because it includes both descendants of American slavery and immigrants of African descent who came to the US from a continent other than Africa. "Black" is more inclusive because it creates a connection between people who look similar in terms of skin color, even if they did not grow up in the US. I also prefer these terms to not be hyphenated with "-American" at the end, because some perceive hyphenation to be a barrier to being fully "American." If you listen to singer, songwriter, and producer Smokey Robinson in a 2022 ABC News interview, you will understand why terminology matters.

"White" or "white," "Black" or black"? I use the capitalized version of each word throughout the book, unless quoting a source in which the words were not capitalized.

"Difference" or "variation"? I avoid using the word "different" to describe people because "different" implies there is a reference group (White people?) against which all others are compared. I use the words "human variation" and similar derivatives wherever possible because humans vary, and human variation is normal.

Off You Go!

The rest of this book will accompany you on an empowering journey to infuse inclusion into your business strategies, organizational culture, and leader behavior. My promise is that by the end of the book, you will feel less frustrated and more confident about handling this challenge.

My client Bill is the CEO of a financial services organization, and he is one of my favorite clients. He called in late 2020 to say, in an atypically halting voice, that he wanted to do more to support his employees after thinking about the social injustices that were driving public protests. Employees had become vocal in sharing their experiences at work, and some of what they shared was alarmingly negative. How did he not know, he wondered? His corporate board, which was usually stoic, had become animated. Not only did they want their employees to have a positive experience, but they did not want to see employee mistreatment stories popping up on social media. And managers were wringing their hands because Bill had not (yet) addressed these issues.

I gave Bill a virtual hug, shared my REDI 10/4 model, and then helped him quickly collect employee feedback to pilot his actions. When he stepped out a couple of weeks later with a clear and empathetic message, his managers were grateful. They now had a North Star guiding their responses. We later implemented a series of information-sharing and education sessions to connect all employees and make them part of building the new experience they desired. Bill went from "deer-in-the-headlights" to "stoked" in a matter of months. Employees sang his praises, and he became more confident about these issues.

This wasn't a "one and done" thing, though. Duke University and Columbia Business School professor, world-ranked communication coach, and thought leader Dorie Clark advises in her book *The Long Game* that transformative change requires a mix of strategic patience and rethinking failure to achieve the goal. Inclusion strategy requires a long-game approach too. Meaningful change requires intentional and persistent action from leaders. REDI strategy must be placed at the core of a business strategy and the organization's cultural expectations. This is how leaders can make corporate America better, one employee at a time.

EXECUTIVE SUMMARY

- George Floyd's and Breonna Taylor's killings illuminated racial injustice and disparities in the US as never before.

- Stakeholders, especially employees, expect business leaders to address these issues.

- Since persistent racial segregation has isolated Americans from people who do not look like them, leaders may need to study history and current social trends to understand these new leadership expectations.

- Only when leaders infuse REDI (respect, equity, diversity, and inclusion) into the core of their business strategy will they drive the kind of meaningful change that employees and other stakeholders can see and feel.

- REDI requires a long-game approach.

REDI QUESTIONS

Has the volume of the conversation about race in the workplace become louder in your organization since May 2020? How are these conversations going? What are you doing to support those conversations? What do you need to understand about these issues that you do not today? Would employees and other stakeholders say you have handled these issues effectively?

2

Yesterday Explains Today

. . . .

The past—or more accurately, pastness—is a
position. Thus, in no way can we identify the past as past.
MICHEL-ROLPH TROUILLOT, *Silencing the Past*

MOST AMERICANS live racially segregated lives.
Our neighborhoods, churches, schools, and workplaces are segregated. This segregation that chills
our emotional connections has remained long
after the official end of slavery because it was constructed
and systemically maintained by many forces, including the
US government.

For example, police officers kill about one thousand Americans each year, with Black Americans dying at almost twice
the rate of White Americans, whether they are in high-crime
environments, are violent criminals, or are not. Yet, there is
no consensus that this disparity is a problem. Citizens' opinions about policing tend to split along race lines. This split is
an artifact of segregation.

But George Floyd's case was different. Many previous
public conversations hinted that victims were perpetrators
of their own demise, casting the deceased as "bad people." If

you believed the victims were bad people, it follows that you might not want to know more about their humanity. Some people might think that the Black victims were just doing the "bad things" that Black people do. But in the heart-wrenching video of Mr. Floyd's killing, the inhumanity was undeniable. For a little time, Americans' opinions shifted a little closer to one another, regardless of race—acknowledging anti-Black racism and questioning some policing tactics. To be clear, police officers are essential to the function of our communities. This past holiday season, I hand-delivered a thank-you gift card to a police officer who helped my family. The root issue is not policing itself; the issue is that some police officers, like some other citizens, seem to view people of color as "other." The root cause is this emotional distance that is an artifact of slavery.

Racism Became a Post-slavery, State-Sanctioned "Norm"

On September 22, 1862, about three years before the Civil War ended (on May 9, 1865), President Abraham Lincoln signed the Emancipation Proclamation, ordering that as of January 1, 1863, all slaves should be "forever free." This date marks the official end of slavery, but it was also the start of a new era of anti-Black racism in the US that continues to this day.

President Lincoln granted amnesty to the Confederate States that fought against the United States of America during the American Civil War with the condition that the Confederacy would agree to abolish slavery. Things went in the right direction... for a short while. During Reconstruction, from about 1865 to 1877, many formerly enslaved Black Americans were taught to read and were able to vote, own land, find jobs, move around the country, use public facilities, and hold public office. However, after President Lincoln's assassination in 1865, his successor, Andrew Johnson, tried to return the Southern states to their pre–Civil War status. Although he failed, former Confederates took control of Southern governments, removed elected Black men from political offices, and enabled the Ku Klux Klan and other racist organizations to terrorize Black Americans into submission.

After 1877, most Southern and border states and local governments enacted laws mandating that all people of color, including Black people, be separated from White people in schools, housing, jobs, and public gathering places. These "Jim Crow" laws (named after a White entertainer who ridiculed Black people as he performed in blackface) were enacted not only in the South, but in almost all fifty states. Most of those monstrous laws remained in place until the Civil Rights movement began to chip away at them, starting in the mid-1950s. The repercussions of Jim Crow can be felt across the US to this day.

Jim Crow laws were not a localized, state-level phenomenon; rather, they had federal support. In 1896, the Supreme Court ruled in *Plessy v. Ferguson* that "separate but equal" was the law of the land, effectively legalizing racial segregation across the republic. By the turn of the 1900s, although the formerly enslaved were legally free, racial segregation was legal in most US states.

This race-based segregation affected most aspects of everyday life for the formerly enslaved. Poll taxes disenfranchised Black voters, Black soldiers who fought in both world wars were marginalized, Black innovators were prohibited from filing patents, Black women's bodies were used for scientific research without their knowledge, and interracial marriage was criminalized. During the Jim Crow era, most day-to-day activities in American cities were segregated, including travel, education, and transportation.

The following examples from the Smithsonian National Museum of American History illustrate the completeness of this segregation:

- In Birmingham, Alabama, in 1930, "It shall be unlawful for a negro and white person to play together or in company with each other in any game of cards or dice, dominoes or checkers."

- In Atlanta, Georgia, in 1926, "No colored barber shall serve as a barber to white women or girls."

- In Mississippi in 1920, "Any person... in favor of social equality or of intermarriage between whites and negroes, shall be guilty of a misdemeanor and subject to a fine..."

- In Maryland in 1924, "Any white woman who shall suffer or permit herself to be got with child by a negro or mulatto... shall be sentenced to the penitentiary for not less than eighteen months."

- In Oklahoma in 1915, "The Corporate Commission is hereby vested with power to require telephone companies in the State of Oklahoma to maintain separate booths for white and colored patrons..."

Segregation was also built into real estate transactions. The Supreme Court ruled, in 1917, that bans on the sale of real estate to Black Americans violated provisions of the Fourteenth Amendment. Yet, the Federal Housing Administration maintained underwriting rules that *encouraged* rejecting loan applications from Black applicants and denying mortgage insurance to Black neighborhoods (a practice

Although the 1863 Emancipation Proclamation ended slavery, Black peoples' lives since then have generally continued to be separate from and mostly unequal to the lives of the descendants of those who designed that oppressive system.

known as "redlining"). The effects of redlining are persistent and pernicious.

It was not until 1954, in the landmark *Brown v. Board of Education* ruling, that the Supreme Court finally ruled the doctrine of "separate but equal" unconstitutional. This decision struck down segregation in public schools and was the vanguard of many subsequent legal rulings that made segregation in housing, public accommodations, and higher education unconstitutional. Passage of the Civil Rights Act, in 1964, granted Black Americans the right of equal access in public accommodations (for example, hotels and transportation). The Voting Rights Act of 1965 protected Black Americans from discrimination in the voting process, and Richard and Mildred Loving's landmark 1967 Supreme Court case legalized interracial marriage in every state. Finally, in 1968, the Fair Housing Act prohibited housing discrimination based on race, color, and other human characteristics.

The separation and disparities described above are not natural; they are *intentional* vestiges of slavery and Jim Crow. Although the 1863 Emancipation Proclamation ended slavery, Black peoples' lives since then have generally continued to be separate from and mostly unequal to the lives of the descendants of those who designed that oppressive system. Though now illegal, systemic forces of racism and segregation have conspired to keep Black Americans in a subordinate position in many walks of life, including the workplace, to this day.

Race Murders

Apart from the restriction of access to services, Black Americans have been consistently terrorized. In June 1921, the thriving Black neighborhood in Tulsa, Oklahoma, Greenwood (also known as "Black Wall Street"), was destroyed by a mob of White Americans. They looted and burned the town, destroying about 1,200 homes, churches, schools, and businesses, as well as the hospital and the library. As many as three hundred Black people died in the massacre. The reason? Some White residents had accused a Black man of accosting a White woman. None of these criminal acts has ever been prosecuted or punished.

The Tulsa Race Massacre was not unique. Across America, especially between the 1870s and the 1920s, many Black towns, businesses, churches, schools, and other social institutions were deliberately destroyed.

Only a century has passed since the Tulsa Race Massacre, and only within the last sixty years or so have many of the legally protected discriminatory practices started in the Jim Crow era been ruled unconstitutional. These historical horrors are still vivid for many Black Americans. Yet, segregation and educational cherry-picking have obscured these same facts to people of other races and backgrounds.

Separate and Unequal

As the conversation about the Black experience amplified in the summer of 2020, many Americans said they were just learning about the racial disparities in American life. Many business leaders said they had not previously heard about, nor fully understood, the enormity of the problem. Research shows definitively that race-based disparities persist in education, income and finances, home ownership, and the workplace. Yet, many White Americans do not believe systemic racism still exists in America. Sergio Peçanha from the *Washington Post* points out that "even though white Americans haven't seen an unemployment rate near 15 percent in decades, African Americans have seen it many times—about once a decade over the past 50 years." Tracy Jan, also from the *Washington Post*, noted that "nearly half of black and Hispanic households had a net worth of less than $50,000 in 2016, compared with about a fifth of whites. At the other end of the income spectrum, 15 percent of white households reported a net worth of more than $1 million, compared with about 2 percent of blacks and Hispanics."

Some of the economic and healthcare disparities are startling:

- The net worth of White households is now ten times that of Black households.

- Black American home ownership remains at the same level as it was in the 1960s and decreased in the decade between 2010 and 2020.

- The percentage of Black children living below the poverty line is three times that of White children, and infant mortality for Black infants is more than twice that of White American infants.

- Black women are more likely to receive late or no prenatal care and face nearly three times the risk of pregnancy-related deaths.

By May of 2020, the US was only a few months into the COVID-19 pandemic, but Black Americans were already dying from COVID-19 at disproportionately high rates relative to their representation in the US population. These disparate health outcomes persisted. The Black community was also dealing with dramatic mental health impacts, disproportionate job losses, and other economic losses. According to Lean In's research, Black women were nearly twice as likely (58 percent) as White men (31 percent) to report having been laid off or furloughed or having had their hours and pay reduced because of the COVID-19 pandemic.

The Two Flags

Several of my neighbors have flags that flap dramatically on the flagpoles impaled on their large green lawns. Soon after January 6, 2021, my neighbor hoisted a gigantic flag with stars and stripes, like an American flag, except that the colors were black, white, and navy blue instead of red, white, and blue. I learned that this flag represented the Blue Lives Matter movement, created by retired and active law enforcement officers. Blue Lives Matter devotees advocate that Americans who are convicted of killing law enforcement officers should be sentenced under hate-crime statutes. This flag made me wonder if the proponents also believe that law enforcement should *not* be held accountable when they wrongfully kill a citizen. I didn't know the answer then, but I did eventually get some clarity.

I have an eighteen-by-twenty-four-inch rainbow-colored sign in my front yard that reads, "Hate Has No Home Here." Five raised hands depict, from left to right, a peace sign, an LGBTQ+ heart, a brown protest fist, a Black Lives Matter heart, and a "White" protest fist. My sign is a way of saying that I advocate for Black Americans and any other marginalized or subordinated group. Does my support for Black Lives Matter mean I don't value and support law enforcement? It does not, but my neighbor might not know that!

There is a large gap
between the reality of the Black
experience in America and
how Americans of other races
perceive that experience.

"I have second thoughts about putting that sign in my yard," I told my best friend. "What if I offend a neighbor? What if someone steals the sign, or eggs my house? What if someone confronts me?" I twisted myself into knots, but I put the sign up anyway; race-based fear is exactly the thing I need to fight against.

These two signs symbolize a gap of understanding and experience that can sometimes feel intractable. My neighbor may misinterpret my flag, just like I might misinterpret his. We both have the right to put up these flags, although to me, the two flags represent non-equivalent values. The flag in my yard is meant to convey inclusion. To me, the flag with the navy-blue line conveys exclusion. But, my neighbor might disagree. He might believe that my flag is the one that conveys exclusion.

We are at a point in America where we have taken "sides" and neither side really knows what the other is thinking. Therein lies the rub. For me to understand what my neighbor feels and how he wants to be supported, I would have to talk directly to him. And I did it... eventually... after a few weeks of hemming and hawing. Guess what he said: "I don't know what you are talking about. I have never seen your sign!"

I laughed. "You mean I went to all that effort to figure out where to place my sign so it would be noticed, but in a non-threatening way... and you never ever noticed?"

He then told me about his flag. "I am a retired law enforcement officer," he said. "I have seen colleagues die in the line of duty. I cry each time a law enforcement officer is killed. I need to stand up for my boys!" By the way, I think he will also stand up for "girls."

I get that! I would probably do the same thing—if I walked in his shoes.

I still don't like my neighbor's flag. But I respect it.

I think my neighbor respects my flag too. At the very least, we now wave at each other as we drive through the neighborhood. The simple act of reaching out helped to bridge the gap.

The Price of Segregated Living

This chapter has been all about the forces that have brought Americans to a point in history where we live segregated lives. Segregation costs us a lot: we misunderstand each other, we distrust each other, and we avoid each other. We also hesitate, like I did, to reach out and act in ways that can shrink the gap.

But as an executive, you don't have a choice. You must lead all employees, so you must provide leadership to help others understand these realities so you can make sure all employees in your organization have an equal chance to thrive. My personal journey of inclusion is not dissimilar to yours. We each need an Inclusion MBA: a Mindset for inclusion and a willingness to take Bold Action. Only then can we bridge the gap, emerging as inclusion role models for those around us. The next three sections of the book detail the Inclusion MBA model, beginning with Mindset.

EXECUTIVE SUMMARY

- Slavery and Jim Crow in the US created systems that perpetuated systemic disparate treatment of Black Americans based on race and ethnicity.

- Systemic racism has resulted in disparate outcomes by race and ethnicity in many aspects of life, including education, healthcare, home ownership, and workplace experiences.

- Racial segregation has aggravated these disparities and made it difficult for Americans to know and understand the connection between these historical facts and Black Americans' current experiences.

- Business leaders can help eliminate race-based workplace disparities by listening to and connecting with employees of all races.

REDI QUESTIONS

How well informed are you about the history and current social patterns in the lives of the employees in your organization and in the larger available workforce? Is it important for you to have clarity about these issues? If so, about which topics would you like to learn more? How can you get those insights? Who can help you get those insights? Will you reach out to those people to get what you need to build your understanding and enhance your leadership effectiveness?

PART TWO

MINDSET

RETHINK WHAT
YOU BELIEVE

Inclusion Reframe #1: Mindset

People vary. Human variation is normal.

3

The Diversity and Inclusion Imperative

. . . .

There can be a huge disconnect between what
executive leaders think about the prevalence
and root causes of diversity and inclusion issues
versus the reality of those experiencing bias.
LAWRENCE HAMILTON, interview with the author

LOVE DIGGING AROUND in employee opinion data.
This is how I came to know, for a fact, that employees
from traditionally underrepresented groups have very different experiences at work than their White colleagues. It
is also how I figured out, many years ago, about the disconnect between what these employees experience at work and
the C-suite's understanding of those experiences. The daily
experiences of many chief executives and C-suite incumbents may be dissimilar to the lives of those you lead, because
of the segregation we discussed in the previous chapter. This
makes it difficult for leaders to recognize the pervasiveness of
overt and unconscious acts of exclusion that people of color
face every day in the workplace.

Marian Croak, Google's vice president of engineering, told this story. Once after being hit by a car, the responding police officer's first question was, "Have you fled bail?" He assumed that, because she was Black, she must have done something to provoke the negative outcome he was seeing! After that interaction, Croak endeavored to never do anything a police officer might misinterpret as threatening. Years later, when responding to an active shooter at her workplace, police officers instructed her to exit her office with her arms raised. Croak was afraid to do it, fearful that that the officers might, as before, misidentify her as "the problem" and respond accordingly.

Croak's reaction might seem extreme to some, but it seems very reasonable to me. I, and so many other Black people in America, experience similar fears and react in similarly defensive ways while interacting with authority figures in charged situations. We do this at work, too, out of fear of being misidentified as "troublemakers."

"Don't Show the CEO!"

For several years I advised the C-suite of a global multi-industrial company how to enhance day-to-day employee experience. In this company the CHRO reported directly to the CEO, and the CDO reported to the CHRO. The CDO wanted to understand if there were patterns of variability in employee experience as a function of certain human characteristics, but the CHRO did not want us to call out that variability when we talked to the CEO. She wanted the CEO to believe that her team was having a very positive impact on employee experience and that most employees were having a great experience.

Since the CHRO controlled the survey data collection and reporting, each year she directed my firm to create a "separate" REDI report, showing employee experience data broken out by key demographics such as race, ethnicity, and gender. That report showed, consistently, that employees of color, especially Black women, were having decidedly less-positive experiences than their colleagues. But the C-suite never saw that report. It was designated "For Human Resources Use Only." No wonder these patterns of disparate experience festered over time.

It was a head-scratching mystery. *Why* didn't the CHRO redress this deteriorating situation? She did not want to ruffle feathers. The CEO seldom asked about REDI matters, so the CHRO seldom brought them up to him or the rest of the C-suite. Instead, she tried to "handle it" within HR. REDI topics were never fully explored. As a result, the C-suite never fully understood the variations in the employee experience until the volume about the issue got loud in the broader community. At that point, the C-suite had to pay attention, but they were caught flat-footed—lacking the insights, perspective, and historical and contextual understanding to lead agile and meaningful change.

CEOs Need to Lead REDI

As business strategist David Lancefield and I explained in a *Harvard Business Review* article, the CEO, the C-suite, and the corporate board of directors must lead REDI for an organization to make meaningful progress. However, if your experiences in and outside of work follow the segregated pattern that is the norm in America, it is hard to define and measure "meaningful" REDI progress. It is difficult to build and lead an inclusive organization without first understanding the experiences of those who have been traditionally excluded.

The awkward conversations I had with colleagues in June of 2020 let me know that they were learning about the true Black experience in America for the first time. I cannot adequately explain how it felt to wake up one day and realize that I and people who look like me had been so unnoticed, so invisible, to some. It stung to hear, "I did not know...!" It stung when some corporations, *for the very first time in history*, checked to see if people of color were represented in their marketing. For the second time in its history, Johnson & Johnson put out a line of bandages, "Band-Aid Brand Ourtone," designed to match multiracial skin tones. It is good to have bandages in a wider range than just the "flesh" tone of yore, but did the product need an "other" special name? Only the marketing experts know for sure!

Many depictions of Black Americans on television and the internet are not representative; they tend to present us either as aggressors (often under duress in law enforcement interactions) or as witless people to be pitied. It is true that many Black Americans who face a daily struggle for survival sometimes make desperate choices for the sake of survival. However, as discussed in Part One of this book, many people who must make those stark choices have never had equal access to the American Dream. It is possible for a Black American to choose a straight and narrow path, use any available resources to seek opportunity, and *yet* find more doors closed than open.

Most Black Americans are descendants of enslaved laborers and, post-Emancipation, of domestics, field hands, and janitors. Their parents worked hard but often did not have equal access to education, healthcare, nutrient-rich food, and

It is difficult to build and
lead an inclusive organization
without first understanding the
experiences of those who have
been traditionally excluded.

housing. Today many of their children, grandchildren, and great-grandchildren may still not have equal access to the promise of American opportunity. Some may be working in your company today. And some of them are marginalized at work, on top of all their other challenges. It will take intentional acts of noticing to see these patterns, understand these human experiences, and create solutions to counter their impact on your employees.

Your Opportunity to Hear as Never Before

These employees want you, as the leader of your organization, to create an environment in which they do not face systemic hindrances, have opportunities to pursue their career aspirations and express their opinions and experiences, and are supported by their managers.

The challenge is that, until now, the daily experience of Black American employees has been hidden, misunderstood, and underestimated. Black employees don't usually talk to coworkers or managers about our experiences at work; it has never been safe to do so. Instead, we share our triumphs and our hurt feelings with our friends and loved ones, outside work. We ask our friends, "How could the leaders who run this organization not realize what is really going on here? Managers and coworkers treat us poorly, and no one seems to care!" These conversations often end with stoic pronouncements such as, "It is what it is." Why bother butting our heads against an immovable wall?

This sense of helplessness to drive change in organizational life is based on patterns we have observed over time—and which are supported by research. Consider the responses to a study I conducted in June 2019, based on data from 1,267 US employed respondents. Fifty-one percent were female, most were between the ages of thirty-six and sixty-four, and 6 percent identified as Black or African American. One survey question asked, "What is something that your company's leaders do not understand about your experience as an employee?" Below are some representative responses from Black respondents:

- I am regularly mistreated at work, but who am I going to tell? If I complain to HR, they are just going to tell my manager (who is often the source of the mistreatment), and he will make my life so miserable that I will have to quit!

- Is it my imagination or do people of color seldom get into the client-facing jobs in the organization?

- Why are so few of the salespeople Black? They make the "big bank," but no matter what I do, I never get selected for one of those jobs.

- Why are so few of the leaders in my company Black?

- Why do companies keep asking us to refer candidates for employment and then fail to follow up with the people we refer?

- Why is it taking so long for me to get selected for a promotion, even though I have all the qualifications they are asking for?

Some of the historical silence may also be because Black employees have learned that too much attention is not a good thing. For example, Black women, especially, are criticized for being too loud or "aggressive," but are simultaneously ignored and overlooked when we achieve. Sociologists call this the "invisibility paradox." As a result, we tend to keep our heads down at work. Unfortunately, a heads-down strategy is the opposite of what is needed to get ahead when business is moving at digital speed. This coping behavior is "rational" in that it allows us to avoid perceived dangers at work, but it is also self-defeating.

Black employees began to speak up more in the summer of 2020 because the dam had burst and they could no longer suppress the workplace frustrations they had hidden for fear of backlash and reprisal. By speaking up now, we hope that leaders will learn by listening and then act to ensure that another generation of employees of color is not exposed to the level of race-based trauma that many of us have consistently endured at work.

What do I mean by "race-based trauma"? In 2000, University of Michigan researchers Drs. David Williams and Ruth Williams-Morris published a comprehensive overview of the research regarding the connection between racism and mental health outcomes among African Americans. Then, in 2019, the American Psychological Association published a special issue of *American Psychologist* dedicated to this subject, pointing out that racial trauma, unlike posttraumatic stress disorder, is ongoing, and involves both individual and collective exposure for People of Color and Indigenous individuals (POCI). The definition of racial trauma in that publication came from the pioneering work of Columbia University's Dr. Robert T. Carter, who codified racial trauma to mean reactions of POCI to dangerous events and real or perceived experiences of racial discrimination.

Employees of color need not wait for corporate America to acknowledge our traumas; we can find new, healthy ways to care for ourselves so these traumas do not scar us for life. But leaders also have an opportunity—an opportunity to listen courageously, and to make leadership decisions based on the fullness of all employees' experiences, and not just on the experiences of a chosen few. This is a chance for leaders to see, hear, and support employees of color as never before.

Build Inclusive Workplaces So All Can Thrive

Stakeholders, including employees and investors, are looking for a new kind of corporate leadership to address the race-based disparities that affect employees. These expectations are being expressed at a time when corporate leadership is also challenged by workforce disruptions, supply chain disruptions, and business model disruptions caused by the COVID-19 pandemic.

Although COVID has had a profound effect on how businesses operate, these new leadership expectations are being driven by even larger forces, many of which preceded the pandemic. For twenty-two years, since 2001, the Edelman organization has been studying trust in institutions globally and reporting their insights in the Edelman Trust Barometer. In 2021, Edelman reported that, for the first time, Americans viewed business as the only institution with both the competence and ethics to deal with society's current ills. Concomitant with that expectation, 86 percent of employees said they wanted CEOs to speak out about societal challenges, including racial justice. The 2022 Edelman results were similar, with business still most trusted (unchanged from 2021), while trust in government, non-governmental organizations, and media declined. The 2022 report also indicated that societal fears were on the rise, with 57 percent of Americans worried about experiencing prejudice or racism—a six-point increase from 2021! Another force is the global movement, codified by the United Nations Sustainable Development

Goals (SDGs), which challenges leaders to balance profit with common good. Third, the future leaders of America, Generation Z, born after 1996, are very concerned about social issues; many believe racial inequality will be a top problem for their generation unless leaders step up to fix it. And the final push, which may be the most influential, is coming from investors.

Americans want CEOs to lead on social issues

Political economist Francis Fukuyama defined societal trust as "the expectation that arises within a community of regular, honest, and cooperative behavior, based on commonly shared norms, on the part of other members of that community." According to Edelman's 2021 report, trust is now based on how well people "believe institutions get things done and whether they do the right thing." To be trusted, institutions must enable their stakeholders to co-create solutions, and their operations must be transparent.

CEOs can act for the "common good"

This landscape of the Black experience came into sharp relief in corporate spaces around the same time that business leaders were focusing on the seventeen United Nations SDGs. The SDGs were adopted by all UN member states (including the US) in 2015 to cover a myriad of social needs, including education, health, social protection, job opportunities, climate change, and environmental protection.

One of these SDGs, Goal 10, "Reduced Inequalities," was created because "inequalities based on income, sex, age, disability, sexual orientation, race, class, ethnicity, religion, and opportunity continue to persist across the world." Goal 10.2 specifies, "By 2030, empower and promote the social, economic and political inclusion of all, irrespective of age, sex, disability, race, ethnicity, origin, religion or economic or other status." This SDG addresses discrimination and inequality in the workplace.

The Business Roundtable is an organization whose members are CEOs of some of America's largest companies. In its August 2019 "Statement on the Purpose of a Corporation," the roundtable proclaimed that "corporations exist to promote an economy that serves all Americans." That statement was controversial for its stance that all stakeholders (shareholders *and* customers, employees, suppliers, and communities) should benefit from the work of corporations. This model of stakeholder primacy was a meaningful departure from the traditional shareholder primacy model that emerged from Milton Friedman's writings. Many roundtable members said this compelling statement simply codified their company's existing values and intentions. Since that statement was drafted, the roundtable's membership has grown, an indication that this pivot to "common good" or "purpose-driven" governance is taking root.

This human-centered social justice perspective also clarifies for leaders that REDI is vital because all employees need to feel valued and secure as they do their jobs supporting business performance. That is very different than the traditional business-case framing for REDI work. In June 2020, the roundtable upped its game, creating a Special Committee to Advance Racial Equity and Justice. Doug McMillon, Walmart president and CEO and Business Roundtable chairman, wrote, "Business Roundtable CEOs do not have all the answers. But we are committed to doing our part to listen, learn, and to use our collective influence and scale to advance racial justice and equal opportunity for all Americans." Tim Ryan, US chair of PwC, has been ringing this bell for many years. In addition to his exemplary REDI leadership within

PwC, he founded the CEO Action for Diversity & Inclusion initiative in 2017—with over two thousand signatories, now the largest CEO-driven business organization focused on advancing diversity and inclusion in the workplace.

There is a new business bottom line. As Aspen Institute Business and Society Program founder and executive director Judy Samuelson wrote in her book *The Six New Rules of Business*, "When public interest and business needs are aligned, extraordinary change is possible."

Generation Z is not about the status quo

Generation Z (often called "Gen Z"), born between 1997 and 2012, is all about breaking the rules—or making their own. According to the Pew Research Center, this generation in America is more racially and ethnically diverse than any other. About 25 percent are Hispanic, 14 percent Black, and 6 percent AAPI. Deloitte says these employees judge organizations not just on the quality of their products and services, but also on their ethics and social impact. Sixty-two percent of respondents to a recent Blue Shield of California NextGen Climate Survey ranked racism and social justice as their primary concern, above environment and social change. As a result, Gen Z is driving a shift of the "balance of power" between employer and employee. We could use the adjective "gutsy" to describe Gen Z, because when they care about an issue, they come together (often on social media) to find solutions, and they push for change. Ziad Ahmed, a college-age social activist, sums up his cohort's sentiment: "At the click of a button, we can start a movement."

Glassdoor data indicates that Gen Z candidates' expectations regarding REDI are affecting their decisions about where they will work. Thirty-seven percent of Gen Z job seekers said they would not apply to a company where employee satisfaction ratings varied by ethnic or racial group. We can expect Generation Z to continue to push their REDI expectations. And they will influence the opinions of colleagues and leaders of all generations. This approach may already be spreading. The 2022 Edelman Trust Barometer reported that 44 percent of global respondents *expect* CEOs to shape conversations and policy debates about prejudice and discrimination.

Investors want social justice and common good

Investors, especially institutional investors, are also putting pressure on corporate board nominating and governance committees to drive diversity in board composition. Additionally, although institutional investors are not all of one cloth, many believe their institutions' values and concerns (including about social justice) should influence their investment selections, in addition to profit and risk evaluations. Initially, environmental, social, and governance (ESG) reporting focused on sustainability, but over time the "S" in ESG has gained more attention, including a heightened focus on REDI. Corporations recognize that social justice and environmental sustainability issues have commonalities: the work is urgent; is for the common good; requires strategic, systemic, and continuous action; and is a stakeholder priority.

Corporate board directors are beginning to feel the pressure from these institutional investors who have the power to vote for or against the selection and retention of board directors. As board directors feel this pressure, they are passing it along to CEOs.

ESG metrics are not currently a required part of financial reporting, though a growing number of companies disclose this information in their annual reports or stand-alone sustainability reports. Numerous institutions, such as

You must create and maintain an
environment in which traditionally
underrepresented groups do
not face systemic hindrances and
are unequivocally safe to voice
the injustices they experience.

the Sustainability Accounting Standards Board, the Global Reporting Initiative, and the Task Force on Climate-Related Financial Disclosures, are working on reporting standards to make it even easier for investors to get the ESG data they want. Regulations are coming, with the European Union leading the charge.

Although public disclosure is not yet the norm, asset managers such as BlackRock, Calvert Research and Management, Trillium, and Boston Trust Walden are among the first to take a public stance for disclosure. They are pressuring the corporations in which they invest to publicly disclose data on the gender, racial, and ethnic composition of their workforces. Corporate pioneers in public disclosure include Amazon, General Motors, Goldman Sachs, Morgan Stanley, and PepsiCo.

A "perfect" and commonly accepted method for reporting REDI data does not exist currently, but organizations could repurpose existing tools as a temporary fix. One such tool is the Employer Information Report EEO-1, which was introduced in 1966, after the passage of the Civil Rights Act of 1964. The Equal Employment Opportunity Commission requires all private sector employers with one hundred or more employees to annually submit demographic workforce data that includes race/ethnicity, sex, and job categories. Companies already have this data, but according to JUST Capital, only 11 percent of America's largest corporations disclose intersectional data of the type reported on the EEO-1. Happily, the numbers doing so are increasing.

Companies still have a lot of work to do when it comes to these ESG expectations. However, they are progressing, as more Americans are asking for traditional capitalism to evolve to meet evolving environmental and social realities.

The pressure will grow, and persist, for CEOs to change leadership practices to meet the needs of a changing world.

Increased calls for transparency and accountability

In February 2021, McDonald's Corporation released a trove of its workforce diversity data and announced they would hold executives accountable for meeting specific diversity and inclusion targets by linking 15 percent of executive bonuses to meeting those targets. The related press release stated, "The Company is incorporating quantitative human capital management-related metrics to annual incentive compensation for its Executive Vice Presidents. In addition to financial performance, the Company will measure executives' ability to champion our core values, improve representation within leadership roles for both women and historically underrepresented groups, and create a strong culture of inclusion within the Company." Starbucks Corporation has also started to share its workforce diversity data and is linking executive pay to diversity and inclusion outcomes.

In August 2021, the Securities and Exchange Commission approved a Nasdaq proposal requiring all companies listed on its US exchange to have at least one female director and a director who self-identifies as a member of a traditionally subordinated race or ethnic group or as lesbian, gay, bisexual, transgender, or queer. (Note: At least seventeen states' attorneys general support a lawsuit filed in late 2021 challenging this Nasdaq rule.)

So, there is rising momentum toward public transparency about workforce diversity in US companies. It seems inevitable that all corporations will eventually report these data to satisfy stakeholder calls for REDI executive accountability.

Sports Helped a CEO Understand REDI

CEOs I interviewed told me they often wonder, "Does this REDI stuff belong on my plate? Wouldn't I be better off lying low to see how this all plays out before I jump in? It seems like a no-win situation to me!"

Neil is the CEO of a hospitality business, and I've known him for more than twenty years. He is very comfortable interacting with people from all walks of life. I am not suggesting that Neil has this challenge whipped (he says that, like most CEOs, he is still figuring this all out). However, he is one of the more clear-eyed, honest, and curious leaders about leading inclusion that I know. Neil doesn't seek out conversations about race, nor does he avoid them. And he doesn't think other leaders should wait and see, lie low, or avoid REDI work because they fear failure on the first try. Rather, he recommends that leaders take the time to learn the facts about US history and about what is happening in their own organization (talking directly to employees), and then model the behaviors they want to be commonplace in their companies. And he thinks it's okay (and probably necessary) to ruffle some feathers along the way to make progress on your inclusion goals.

How did Neil develop this perspective? Although educated in a segregated Pittsburgh school system, Neil has interacted with people from various races and backgrounds since grade school. His world grew even more diverse when Neil later became a high-school basketball coach.

"I find that sports have an almost an intrinsic power to unify people," he explained to me. "I have played with African American colleagues since the sixties. We ate lunch together. We went to one another's houses. That is why it is easy for me not to judge someone by their appearance. What matters is what they bring to the table, their personality, their work ethic, and how they will help our organization.

"If you feel uncomfortable communicating with people who do not look like you, you have to get out of your shell. You can't delegate this. You should be sincerely interested in what people need and how you can help them. This will help you, too, because it will make it easier for them to contribute and perform. If you can't look past a person's skin color, then you probably shouldn't be a leader today, because you're not leading everybody, you're only leading a segment."

EXECUTIVE SUMMARY

- Stakeholders (especially employees and investors) are calling for REDI changes, and the rising generation (Generation Z) is pushing for more, and faster, change than prior generations.

- Corporate executives have a unique power to make REDI changes that can enhance the experience of all employees, including those from traditionally underrepresented groups.

- To understand how to enhance the experiences of employees from traditionally underrepresented groups, leaders must connect with all employees.

REDI QUESTIONS

Do you believe that CEOs and other corporate executives should be active participants in making the workplace better when it comes to racism? If you agree with that idea, how might you make it part of your overall leadership vision? If you don't believe in this idea today, do your current beliefs hinder your effectiveness at leading all employees? How are you able to manage your actions to ensure that other leaders and employees do not pick up on your ambivalence about this issue?

4

Understand Your Beliefs about REDI

. . . .

Not everything that is faced can be changed;
but nothing can be changed until it is faced.
JAMES BALDWIN, "As Much Truth as One Can Bear"

STARTED A NEW JOB, and on my very first day, the CEO's husband and baby boy visited the office to celebrate her birthday. I liked the CEO; she was smart, thoughtful, ethical. A trustworthy leader—with a beautiful family as a bonus.

A few months later, on a balmy summer day, I met work colleagues in Philadelphia for dinner. The CEO was there. We were in the "small talk" phase of the meal, and I said, "You have such a beautiful family." She recoiled viscerally, moving so abruptly that the legs of her chair made a muffled scraping sound. Then she said, in a terrified voice, "How do you know *my* family?" I learned from this quick interaction that, from my simple mention of her family, she had perceived me as a threat. I wanted to say, "Look, I am just making small talk here." But I said nothing. I was shocked, disappointed, and hurt. I had tried to communicate in a way that would establish a small connection, and she had rebuffed that effort, putting me in my place. I had forgotten the cardinal rule: you may be "in the team," but being "part of the family" is a whole other thing.

Every time I saw this leader, I remembered that hurt. I had joined the company with great optimism, but the wind came out of my sails when I realized that she saw me as "other." I could no longer see her as a leader, and I could not imagine having a thriving career in her organization. I never told her or anyone else in the company how I felt. Instead, I decided, in that moment, that I would leave the organization. And I did.

Executives are often unaware of the power of their actions. The leader I just mentioned was oblivious to her alienating and disengaging behavior. But to effectively lead *all* employees, leaders must practice REDI. It all starts with self-awareness about your own REDI beliefs.

REDI Anxiety

No matter where my conversations with executives about inclusion strategy start, they inevitably land on one unavoidable issue: how to address REDI in meaningful ways without tearing their organizations apart. The main issue is not usually *what* they should do, but rather the emotions that stop them from acting. Executives labeled these emotions in various ways, including "fear," "anxiety," and "discomfort." Fear and anxiety are distinct, both conceptually and physiologically, although the terms are often used interchangeably. Fear is a present-oriented and short-term response to a *specific* threat, while anxiety is a future-oriented and long-acting response to a *diffuse* threat as you anticipate danger, catastrophe, or misfortune. Anxiety produces tense muscles, rapid breathing, and an increased heart rate. These executives' emotions are anxiety rather than fear. So, let's call it REDI Anxiety!

The leaders I interviewed consistently mentioned three factors that fostered anxiety and inhibited their REDI action:

1 **REDI role uncertainty.** Some executives said they were unsure how to prioritize REDI, because of (1) a lack of clarity about the problem within their organizations and (2) concern that the issue would consume disproportionate time relative to their other obligations. Leaders who expressed this concern believed the issues were worthy of exploration but, rather than focusing on leading the strategy, hoped their "D&I team" would design a strategy and just pull them in when they needed approval to implement it.

2 **REDI dodging.** Some executives expressed discomfort with conversations about social and political issues, including racial justice, in the workplace. According to *Fortune* magazine, as of May 2021, about 50 percent of CEOs said they were reluctant to speak out publicly about these issues. Influential North Carolina entrepreneur and investor Donald Thompson wrote in a 2020 article, "They're worried that one wrong word will further exasperate or alienate their employees, open them to criticism from investors and friends, or be taken out of context by the media." These leaders realize that many employees are not accustomed to talking about race, never mind taking action to address race-based disparities. And they don't want to alienate those who do not support the increased focus on diversity and inclusion!

3 REDI distance. Many leaders I interviewed recognized and acknowledged they did not have experience interacting with people who do not look like them. They also said that their well-intentioned overtures had been received poorly by employees from traditionally subordinated groups. These leaders want to make a positive difference but don't understand life experiences that are dissimilar to their own and don't know where to start.

If you want to overcome REDI Anxiety, you must understand how your own personal experiences affect your REDI feelings today. Only then will you be able to purposefully connect with and lead all your employees, in their many variations.

Inclusive Leaders Need a REDI Mindset

Andrés Tapia and Alina Polonskaia at Korn Ferry have defined the traits (personal characteristics) and competencies (actions) of inclusive leaders. The inclusive traits in their model are authenticity, emotional resilience, self-assurance, inquisitiveness, and flexibility. The behavioral competencies that leaders should master are building interpersonal trust, integrating diverse perspectives, optimizing talent, applying an adaptive mindset, and achieving transformation. The authors also argue that biography matters. They believe that each leader (and each employee) interprets their current experience based on their past experiences and socialization. Leaders whose social experiences have been diverse are more likely to see the world from a variety of perspectives and to effectively lead others who do not look like them or who have had different experiences than theirs. Conversely, those who lack that breadth of human experience must put in extra effort to effectively lead a diverse team.

Dr. Carol Dweck made a seminal contribution to the study of human motivation through her research-based concept of "growth mindset." People who have a growth mindset believe that, through dedication and hard work, they can develop the capabilities they need to accomplish any goal. Dweck said they "worry less about looking smart and ... put more energy into learning." In subsequent research, Dweck and her team determined that, even if not born with it, one can cultivate a growth mindset to generate "novel solutions to new and old problems." Growth mindset encourages problem solvers to "draw connections" across unfamiliar ideas.

A growth mindset is likely an advantage for solving any business problem and, since it can be cultivated, might be particularly useful for building inclusive leadership behaviors. A "REDI Mindset" would require one more element, in addition to curiosity and connection. That element is *comfort*—a willingness to relax and create ease when thinking about and interacting with people whose experiences vary from your own.

When that leader at the dinner table recoiled in reaction to my small talk, I instantly inferred that she did not have a REDI Mindset. She wasn't curious, seemed to be avoiding connection, and appeared uncomfortable. I wondered how I could have a successful career in an organization whose leader was so uncomfortable in my presence.

We judge a person to be *consciously* biased when their actions and speech indicate disdain or dislike for another person based on human characteristics including race, gender, and physical or neurological capabilities, for example. We might call such a person racist, sexist, or ableist.

I do not think the leader who recoiled from me was consciously biased. Rather, her reaction seemed unconscious and automatic. Remember, this is a woman I mostly admire and who most would agree is decent and honorable. I am sure she was oblivious to the emotional hurt I felt from that interaction and probably does not remember it. That is because the culprit that caused her to recoil is most likely implicit (unconscious), interpersonal bias.

Implicit (or Unconscious) Bias

Over time, like the psychologist I am, I began to think of my life in two phases: the pre-US phase and the US phase. In the pre-US phase, I worked hard and went above and beyond, and those behaviors were judged to be successful. In the US phase, I learned that working hard and going above and beyond are not necessarily enough. And I learned that sometimes, though eminently prepared, I must gird myself with extra layers of psychological armor to survive challenges that seem at their core to be asking, "Why are you here?"

Yale psychologist Dr. John Dovidio "wrote the book" on how implicit bias affects thinking, feeling, and responding to others, depending on their membership in the same social group. His research shows that contemporary racism is subtle, often unintentional, and unconscious, and that its perpetrators believe they are not prejudiced. This is called "aversive racism." Aversive racists do not discriminate directly or openly. They act in ways that can be justified on some other basis but, nevertheless, discriminate against the target group. Aversive racists tend to perceive the same behaviors or events, even events that are clearly discriminatory, differently than

A REDI Mindset uses curiosity, connection, *and* comfort to power understanding of people whose lived experiences vary from your own.

those in the subordinate group who are victims of the discrimination. They also tend to have anxiety around people of color, which is revealed by avoidance and social awkwardness.

This combination of avoidance and social awkwardness is the hallmark of many workplace interactions between leaders and employees of color. This is the REDI Anxiety leaders must overcome. Remember that REDI is a respect-first model. For people of color, sometimes REDI Anxiety shows up in a form that looks like disrespect.

The implicit bias being discussed here is pervasive in one-to-one and group workplace interactions; it is an interpersonal bias.

Phil Dixon has studied both human behavior in organizations and neuroscience for decades and is the author of the book *Bias, Racism, and the Brain*, coauthored with Jason Greer. In interviews with me, Phil explained that the brain has two parts, the emotional part, which is on constant alert, and the logical part, which is also ready to respond, but more slowly. Sometimes, when the emotional part perceives a threat, it shuts down the logical part and acts independently. This emotional part of the brain that reduces logical thinking is "driven by biases, habits, and patterns, does not like to change, often behaves irrationally, and is subject to all sorts of other nonconscious influences." (The use here of the term *"non*conscious" is intentional. This is Phil's preference, and it means the same as *"un*conscious," which I use elsewhere.) These forces give rise to responses that suggest implicit bias is driving the visible behavior.

The CEO I mentioned previously was likely unaware of both the thoughts that preceded her action and the action itself. This is what implicit or unconscious bias is all about. The science regarding unconscious bias indicates the following:

- **Experiences matter.** All our experiences—long past, recent past, and present—influence what we believe (and how we act) today.

- **We learn through relationships.** The opinions and behavior we have observed from people around us, especially in the formative stages of our lives, influence our beliefs (and actions) today.

- **Some of what we believe and do is implicit (unconscious).** We do not control everything about our behavior, and sometimes we do not realize what we have done. This is how an employee from a subordinated group might be offended by a leader's actions, while the leader might be unaware they have done something offensive. The CEO's reaction to me during dinner is most likely in that category—implicit, insignificant, and forgettable to her, but explicit, highly resonant, and unforgettable to me.

- **We are less attuned to the invisible than to the visible dimensions of expression.** Our thoughts and feelings are (mostly) invisible to others, while our speech and actions are visible. We like to think that by controlling our speech and actions we control the messages we deliver. However, implicit bias research shows that we also communicate thoughts and feelings of which we are unaware.

- **People make judgments about each other.** During interactions, we judge one another based not only on what we say or do but also on what we infer, which is based on our own lived experiences.

- **An observer's perceptions are out of our control.** What we say or do may not match what others perceive.

- Leaders have an extra burden to anticipate perceptions. For leaders, not only do intentions matter, but how communication (verbal and nonverbal) is *perceived and interpreted* by observers is also critical.

- Employees are the key observers of leaders. I like to say that leaders have a bullseye in the middle of their foreheads. Employees constantly watch everything leaders say and do and constantly interpret both verbal and nonverbal cues to "read the wind" and predict how they will be affected by the leader. Employees also look for clues about how they will be affected by a leader's REDI Mindset (or lack thereof).

Unconscious (and Conscious) Bias Matters, Especially for Leaders

Unconscious bias serves a purpose. Phil Dixon says that if the brain had to consciously process each of the eleven million bits of information it encounters *each second*, we would become paralyzed. These biases and habits are "the brain's way of not having to consciously think about everything all the time ... and are useful shortcuts that become entrenched." Harvard researcher Iris Bohnet puts it this way: "Our minds are stubborn beasts. It's very hard to eliminate our biases ..." Black *and* White people are biased; each of us has a fallible brain. We are all biased because we are humans with human brains. It's as simple as that.

How unconscious bias plays out

When I moved to the US, I was twenty years old, a fully formed young woman. I had come from a place where a lot of people looked like me, and those people were always pushing me forward, expecting the excellence that I delivered. Their emotional support enabled me to move freely, not only in that country but also when I traveled beyond its borders.

When I started living in the US, I realized that some people were not seeing "Gena," they were seeing an avatar called "Black Woman," and they wanted me to fit into that box. Many told me, through their reactions, that they expected me to have low expectations for myself and that their expectations for me were even lower. Many treated me as if they believed I was not as smart or as capable as I am. And it seemed that I was often invisible; people would look through me, ask me to repeat my clearly stated observations, and ask me to justify my presence, especially in business situations.

Hardly a week goes by in which a White person does not relate to me in a way that seems to be asking, "Why are you here?" Just this year I attended a Zoom meeting with a peer group of businesswomen. After the plenary session, we were split into breakout rooms. As soon as I arrived at my assigned room, a White woman said, "I think you are in the wrong room!" Without giving me a chance to respond, she continued, "I am contacting the meeting leader to make sure you are in the right place." And off she went, typing furiously into her cell phone, so she could confirm her belief that I was "out of place." She held up the entire meeting to do this. Meanwhile, I was so shocked that I was (uncharacteristically) speechless. About ten minutes later she announced, "It's okay. I was wrong. You're good! Sorry." This woman did not realize she had embarrassed me in front of my peers, most of whom were meeting me for the first time. This felt like

unconscious bias, like a not-so-subtle act of exclusion. Sometimes, as social anthropologist Dr. Veronica Escalante would
say, we are seeing others through "purple lenses" that discolor what we "see."

A Word about Intentional, Conscious Bias

The main reason a book like mine is necessary is that many
White Americans seem very uncomfortable interacting with
people of color, even in the workplace and when they are
responsible for leading us. We walk into a space and almost
immediately observe weird nonverbal behaviors from those
in the dominant group. Someone might single us out unnec-
essarily for being in the "wrong" space, for our hair, or for
some other random thing that has caught their attention,
even when we enter corporate spaces with friendly smiles
and normative attire. And we have all seen many examples
of overt bias in the media. It is bias when someone calls the
police on a Black birdwatcher, on a group of Black people
grilling in a park, or on a couple of Black men who want to
use a café restroom. Those are acts of conscious, *not* unconscious, bias. And each experience shakes us to the core.

Systemic Bias: Even More Impactful Than Interpersonal Bias

Interpersonal bias and systemic racism, though inextricable,
are not the same thing.

   According to the National Museum of African American
History and Culture, systemic racism "is the overarching
system of racial bias across institutions and society. These

systems give privileges to White people resulting in disadvantages to people of color." The definition ends by providing a most obviously egregious example of systemic bias: the stereotypical depiction of people of color as criminals in mainstream movies and media.

Systemic bias, also called structural bias or structural racism, is even more pervasive, impactful, and misunderstood than implicit and interpersonal bias. Sometimes it operates right under our noses outside the awareness of those who perpetuate it or have the power to change it.

Researchers Drs. Julian Rucker and Jennifer Richeson explain that systemic bias/racism is "critical to preserving perceptions of societal fairness, despite the presence of group-based inequality." In other words, demeaning racial stereotypes, though damaging to those targeted, case the discomfort that might otherwise arise if people were to honestly reflect on the fairness of the structures that create disparate outcomes. These researchers also conclude that many Americans, especially White Americans, do not understand the role of systemic racism because they are exposed to more miseducation than accurate information about systemic bias and its impacts. The recent high-volume debate about Critical Race Theory is a case in point. This miseducation, Rucker and Richeson explain, is why some Americans tolerate "stark levels of racial inequity" while simultaneously professing good intentions.

Pew Research data consistently shows that Black Americans view systemic bias as the primary impediment to our progress, while White Americans focus more on interpersonal bias. Rucker and Richeson point out that it is only when White Americans understand the realities of systemic racism that they begin to perceive social inequality "in a way that is similar to Black Americans' views."

Although it is vital to address both interpersonal and systemic bias in organizations, focusing on the systemic bias will have a faster and more scalable impact.

These are some of the reasons why I advise leaders to focus more effort on understanding and addressing *systemic* manifestations of bias in the workplace than on *interpersonal, implicit* bias. Systemic bias affects *all* people in the system (in the organization), and its effects, though persistent, may not be readily observed or redressed. Although it is vital to address both interpersonal and systemic bias in organizations, focusing on the systemic bias will have a faster and more scalable impact on disparate outcomes than focusing on interpersonal bias.

Examples of systemic bias in the workplace

A leader once told me I was not selected for a promotion because it was not "my turn." I had earned consistently stellar performance reviews, but the leader's decisions about my promotion seemed to be influenced by factors other than my actual performance. Apparently, the performance of the fellow who got the job wasn't a deciding factor either; his peer group regarded him as a slacker! Time in the organization was more highly valued than performance, so the slacker got the job. This decision was mundane systemic bias. If the only people who get promotions are those who have been with an organization for an undefined "x" number of years, high-level jobs will always and only get filled by "insiders." And if the insiders are all from one social group, those who are newer to the organization, the outsiders, will never get promoted.

You might think that this kind of selection bias could not happen in your organization because you base your promotion decisions on managers' performance ratings. However, research clearly shows that performance ratings can be unreliable. They tell you more about the rater's *perceptions* of the ratee than about the ratee's *actual performance*. Organizational psychologist Dr. Kathlyn Wilson is senior lecturer in Human Resources Management and Organizational Behavior at the University of Hertfordshire Business School in the UK. In a 2021 interview, she shared her research that performance raters apply unique mental models when rating people from a race or ethnic group other than their own. Furthermore, when Wilson examined her study participants' responses, she found they often *justified* their ratings based on factors that had nothing to do with the organization's performance criteria! In other words, raters are not necessarily objective when providing performance ratings. These "idiosyncratic rater effects" are one of the primary reasons consulting firm Deloitte completely redesigned its performance management system years ago. And yet, performance ratings are held up in many organizations to justify disparate talent outcomes. The outcomes are often disparate because the tools and processes are biased!

Talent decision making is highly susceptible to systemic bias. However, if you understand how systemic bias works, you can counter its effects in talent and other managerial decision processes, including the criteria used for promotions and access to high-level leadership roles. You can impact these systems by requiring your HR staff to examine the validity of their performance appraisal system to understand if it functions fairly or inadvertently adds bias to the process.

What Can You Do?

Your efforts to build an inclusive organization will be influenced by both conscious and unconscious factors. You may be able to voice the conscious, rational, and logical drivers, but can you verbalize the unconscious, emotional drivers of your feelings and actions?

If you want to make even a dent in the REDI challenge, I encourage you to follow the five-step REDI Action model to process your feelings in preparation for action:

1   Understand what you believe about REDI.

2   Face your REDI Anxieties.

3   Connect with people you currently do not understand.

4   Build your personal **Get REDI plan.**

5   **Model the REDI way** like the organization's primary change agent (which is what you are)!

Awareness of your unconscious biases will help you surface the feelings and behaviors that might unintentionally derail your REDI efforts. You will then be more effective in building and leading an inclusive organizational culture imbued with an emotionally informed perspective to REDI leadership. Author and behavioral scientist Matt Wallaert puts it this way: "Leaders sometimes inadvertently reveal that 'I don't really want to hear it' when it comes to race and gender issues. They promote inhibiting pressures, which make the change behaviors less likely. What a leader really needs to do in a situation that requires change is set up promoting pressures—pressures that make the new behaviors more likely. Leaders must make sure they are not doing the opposite of what they say they want to do!"

Step #1: Understand what you believe about REDI
Dr. W. Brad Johnson is professor of psychology in the department of Leadership, Ethics, and Law at the United States

Naval Academy and a faculty associate in the Graduate School
of Education at Johns Hopkins University. He believes that
"CEOs must articulate *why* REDI work is important on a
personal level before they attempt to implement an enterprise-
wide inclusion strategy. Leaders must be able to communicate, 'What is your personal connection to inclusion and
diversity? Why does this matter to you personally?'"

The **REDI Skin in the Game Warm-Up** that follows will
help you think through what you believe about REDI and
why you believe it. These exercises explore some of your
conscious and unconscious beliefs about understanding,
interacting with, and supporting people of color, including
Black Americans.

If you hold a senior leadership role, your feelings and
beliefs will affect the entire organization. If your feelings
and beliefs naturally support REDI work, that is great. If
your feeling and beliefs lead to only partial support or if, in
your heart, you do not support this work at all, you will have
difficulty leading REDI strategically because you will not
be able to explain your "why" to employees. If your direct
reports detect even a whiff of your resistance, they will
constrain their own change efforts. If employees, potential
employees, or other business partners sense your resistance,
their trust in your organization might be reduced. Candidates
from the full spectrum of human life will not be attracted to
your organization, nor will they stay in it, if they question
your commitment to REDI work.

Your beliefs and feelings may be more visible than you
realize. Are they enhancing or hindering your inclusive leadership? Are you ready to lead the building of an inclusive
culture for your organization?

REDI Skin in the Game Warm-Up

Conscious beliefs exploration: These questions explore your involvement in, and beliefs about, experiences and social and economic circumstances in which races tend to be segregated in the US. These questions are meant to encourage introspection, so there are no right or wrong answers. Answer "Yes" or "No" by writing Y or N in the column to the right of the questions.

Conscious beliefs and experiences	Y or N
I regularly interacted with people of other races than mine in my high school education, other than when they provided services to me or my family.	
I regularly interacted with people of other races than mine in my post-high school education (college, etc.), other than when they provided services to me or my family.	
I regularly interacted with people of other races than mine in jobs I have held before my current role.	
I have a sense of what it feels like, in the US, to be a person whose race is other than my own.	
I understand there are often disparities in access to education, healthcare, and housing in the US based on race/ethnicity.	
I understand there are often disparities in access to employment opportunities in the US based on race/ethnicity.	
Currently, I regularly interact with people of other races than mine at work.	

Conscious beliefs and experiences	Y or N
Currently, I regularly interact with people of other races than mine *outside* work.	
I know what it feels like to be an employee at this company.	
I know what it feels like to be an employee from a traditionally underrepresented group at this company.	
I believe that since I am the CEO, a C-suite member, a board director, or another leader at this company, I have a special responsibility for leading REDI issues here.	
I am ready to play my part in taking ownership of REDI issues in this company.	

What do you think? Do your responses to these questions suggest that you are familiar and comfortable with the experiences of people who do not look like you?

Unconscious beliefs exploration: Now it's time to explore the unconscious aspects of your feelings and actions. Be candid with yourself. Again, there are no right or wrong answers, and your responses are just for your own use.

Recall a scenario in a business situation where you acted out an unconscious bias. Perhaps you avoided eye contact with a person of color or turned your body to eliminate any potential contact between you and that person. Perhaps you said something that assumed facts about an employee's cultural background, economic status, or education level based on their appearance, without knowing the reality of it. Perhaps you excluded a person from a business event where their job and expertise should have been represented because you felt awkward in their presence due to their race or ethnicity. Remember, the action was unconscious, so you may have to dig deep to recognize it. Once you have, answer the following:

- *Why* did you do what you did?

- Do you think the person *noticed* what you did?

- If the person did notice, how do you think they *felt?*

- How do you think that exclusion influenced that person's feelings about *you?*

- How do you think that exclusion influenced that person's feelings about *their job?*

- How do you think that experience influenced that person's *feelings* about working at your company?

- How do you think that exclusion affected that person's *effectiveness* in doing their job?

- What *different outcome* might you seek the next time you find yourself in a similar situation at work?

- What could you do differently, to get a *positive outcome* for you and the other person, next time you find yourself in a similar situation?

Now, considering your responses to the questions in both the conscious and unconscious beliefs sections of the REDI Skin in the Game Warm-Up, are you REDI, or are you feeling some REDI Anxiety?

Note: The REDI Skin in the Game Warm-Up is also available for download at leadinginclusion.com.

Step #2: Face your REDI Anxieties

If you experience REDI Anxiety, you are not alone. Most of the C-suite executives I interviewed were brutally honest, admitting that they have some anxiety about wading into REDI work. Below is a summary of the most common anxiety themes from those conversations.

Fluctuating emotions (confidence and anxiety). You vacillate between optimism and moments of self-doubt. You want to create something sustainable but hesitate because you are unsure what *the right thing* is. You worry your actions will not resonate with employees and fear alienating some employees. You worry about backlash and feel like you're damned if you do, damned if you don't.

Varied and unknown employee expectations. Most employees expect progress, but everybody has a different definition of the content and pace of that progress. Sometimes employees evaluate progress not only on what is happening within your company, but compared to what their friends are experiencing at other companies.

Communicating the new(er) culture of inclusion. You know that your company has some catching up to do regarding REDI work. Yet, you need to hire new people even though the new inclusive culture is still a work in process. You don't want to seem hypocritical, nor do you want to give an unrealistic job preview, pretending that all is well. You want new leaders you hire to start from day one with a clear understanding of your inclusion expectations so their behavior can model the new way.

Cascading REDI expectations. You want all leaders and managers to understand your inclusion goals, but getting the message down into the organization is neither easy nor quick.

Guilt about past actions. You worry that things you or other leaders have done might not have been inclusive, but you are unsure what to do to remedy that so you and your employees can move forward.

So, what can a leader do? You can either freeze under the burden of these anxieties, or you can use them to spur yourself to action. Freezing is not an option. Steps 3 to 5 in the REDI Action model will provide more guidance, but you should constantly seek to understand all employees' perspectives. Employees don't expect you to be perfect when it comes to REDI; rather, they are impressed with leader honesty and vulnerability about the things you are still learning that will make you a better leader. You might also seek the guidance of a professional inclusion strategist or coach to process your feelings and derive meaningful actions for moving forward. You need to face these REDI Anxieties to overcome them.

Step #3: Connect with people you currently do not understand

When employees feel connected to their managers and to the organization, they are more engaged and inspired at work. That is why you must find ways to connect with employees. Do all you can to understand the experience of employees who have been traditionally subordinated.

There are many ways you can connect with and learn from a wide range of people. Some of the actions listed below will seem obvious, but keep in mind that a leader's actions have direct and outsized influence on employee experience. In getting back to basics, you can connect with employees on a deeper level.

Reduce social distance to build empathy. As Dr. Tiffany Jana notes, the lack of proximity between leaders and those whom you might think of as "different" creates "a lack of empathy." The American Psychological Association defines empathy as understanding a person from their frame of reference rather than one's own. There is a large body of psychological science showing that empathy can overcome prejudice. As futurist Sophie Wade points out, empathy helps create connection and understanding that drives business outcomes. There are few substitutes for proximity when it comes to building empathy. So, put yourself in places where people don't look like you. Make sure your recruiters and marketing team are sponsoring and participating in professional events and organizations where they will encounter diverse participants.

One of the paradoxical outcomes of slavery and Jim Crow is that, out of necessity, Black Americans created parallel retail, educational, financial, religious, and social organizations to get the resources and services to which they were denied access in the broader community. That is why we have Black hairdressers, colleges and universities, sororities and fraternities, banks, and churches. Those institutions are usually "safe spaces" for Black people, although, in 2022, some of them were targeted by bomb threats!

If you study these institutions, you will uncover the creativity, intellect, and determination that are hallmarks of the communities they serve. The students, clients, and customers of these organizations could become employees, suppliers, and partners to your organization if you get to know them and if they trust that your REDI actions are sincere.

Build your connecting muscle. Approach connecting with unfamiliar people with the same intentionality you use for other strategic challenges. Alisa Cohn, author and executive coach to start-up executives, acknowledges that this is not easy, but she says it is doable. The key, she recommends, is to realize that the person on the other end is likely as apprehensive as you, especially since you likely have more traditional power than they. She advises that you recognize when your own emotions are getting in the way, but power through anyway. Once you make the first step, subsequent steps will be easier.

Since it might take a minute to warm up the conversation, have two or three questions in your back pocket to start. You might think that asking questions makes others perceive you as lacking knowledge and less competent than you are. However, the opposite is true. Research indicates that leaders gain, rather than lose, relationship-building credibility when they ask questions!

Alisa suggests that even if the conversation loses steam, you haven't lost anything; rather, you've built your muscle for approaching strangers in the future. Tune in to that feeling of concern or squeamishness in your stomach, throat, or chest, she recommends, and ask yourself, "What am I afraid of? What is this feeling telling me?" Since you are likely afraid of being judged, Alisa advises unpacking those feelings and practicing new behaviors. She says you can tell that little voice inside of you, "Yeah, I'm glad you're here. Come with me. We're going on a journey that will make our lives richer." As you can tell, she believes that *optimism and goodwill* are key.

Alisa is right! Researchers have recently discovered that conversations between strangers can be highly satisfying. The counterintuitive secret to positive outcomes is to have deep, rather than shallow, conversations! So, stay away from "Where did you grow up?" kinds of questions, and aim higher, with questions like, "What is something for which you are grateful?" These are the kinds of questions that will create more satisfying connections with strangers.

Connect and listen. Board member, investor, REDI leader, and general counsel Tricia Montalvo Timm says that in her experience, when leaders hear the stories of their colleagues of color first-hand, they are transformed. Once you start listening and learning, you will want to act. Tricia says three simple words, "Tell me more," can initiate a powerful dialogue, revealing systemic patterns in your organization you had not previously noticed.

Intentionally build bridging capital. I mentioned Dorie Clark previously when talking about her long-game perspective regarding meaningful transformation. Dorie is also expert at helping others connect. In an interview with me, she offered this advice: "[Dr.] Robert Putnam's concepts of *bonding capital* and *bridging capital* are useful for thinking about this. Bonding social capital develops *within* a group or community, whereas bridging social capital is formed *between* social groups (for example, social class, race, religion, etc.). To have a successful professional or personal network, you need both kinds of capital. Of course, it's much easier to build bonding capital than bridging capital, but the payoff for building both is significant!" Dorie acknowledges it's reasonable to assume we *don't* have things in common with people who look different from us. Nevertheless, she says, "If we put in a little effort, we can find the commonalities, even if we have to dig for them." Those commonalities will drive both connection and empathy.

Dine together. Consider starting with one of the simplest yet most effective things you can do—share a meal (or many) with your colleagues. Author and entrepreneur Chris Schembra believes that gratitude is the foundation for all strong connections and relationships. Chris founded the organization 7:47 to help leaders facilitate connections with and

between their employees through in-person and virtual din-
ing experiences that are focused on gratitude. At each event,
each participant is asked, "If you could give credit or thanks
to one person in your life whom you don't give enough credit
or thanks to, who would that be?" People ponder this question while eating, and participants become more empathetic
and trusting of each other. Empathy can help employees feel
seen. As Chris put it, "If leaders just create the space to listen
to the needs of the people they serve, they will retain their
top talent and attract even more."

Play together. Simple tools like card games can be useful for
getting people together to talk about REDI issues. Games like
#CultureTags by Eunique Jones Gibson, So Cards by Miguel
Luis, and Over Coffee by Gena Scurry can be useful conversation starters. Once you get warmed up, the conversations
can become less structured and more organic.

Use employee opinion surveys. Although the intimate connections recommended above are crucial, you also need
scalable solutions for learning about employee experiences.
Employee opinion surveys are among the most effective and
efficient tools at your disposal. They can help reduce the risk
of faulty decision making caused by over-relying on the opinions of just your inner circle or the loudest voices in the room.

If you decide to use surveys in your REDI journey, remember these four rules. Only do so if you (1) are prepared to hear
the answers, (2) are prepared to act on the employee feedback, (3) are willing to share the results of the survey with
the employees who provided the feedback, and (4) will survey
employees regularly and not just as a one-shot activity.

Note: Employee opinion surveys are covered in greater
detail in Chapter 10.

Step #4: Build your personal Get REDI plan

Now that you have done some self-reflection and explored potential ways to connect with people you want to know better, this is a good time to start thinking about how you will use your new perspective to steer the larger organization. You need a plan, a Get REDI plan. It's a preliminary personal strategy that will inform your eventual REDI organizational strategy. Here are a few prompts to help with this step.

Create a personal REDI advisory team. This is not a process-oriented working group; rather, the main purpose is for the members to give you the ideas, perspectives, and feedback you might not get from your usual inner circle. Some of their insights may come from data, but many will come from life experience. You need both. The members don't have to come together in caucus; you can work with them individually or in small groups. But this is the group with which you will share your REDI goals, fears, and concerns. Ideally some of these individuals will come from outside your core leadership team. Try to include employees from levels and parts of the organization with which you typically have little contact. You might even include a few people from outside the organization.

Recruit reverse mentors. Regularly interact with and learn from younger employees across the spectrum of human variation. Engage them as reverse mentors with whom you check in periodically to get the pulse of the organization.

Educate yourself about the demographic characteristics of your workforce. Examine employees' opinions by race, ethnicity, gender, LGBTQ+ status, ability, and any other dimensions of variation that matter in your organization. Further, examine the data by location, leader, job level, category,

Employees do not expect
you to be perfect when it
comes to REDI. Vulnerability
can work to your advantage.

and other ways in which employees are segmented in your business. If yours is a global organization, ensure that you receive data broken out by countries/regions, in ways that are culturally meaningful in those locations. For example, in the US we typically use the US Census race designations, plus ethnicity. In the UK, race and ethnicity groupings are more complex—and contentious. Use the groupings that are appropriate for the part of the world in which you are doing business. Do not try to use US classifications or interpretations in other parts of the world.

Consume varied media. Add new content sources to your regular reading/listening list. Read online newsletters and newspapers or listen to podcasts and the like that provide a balanced perspective on social issues.

Continue your self-education. Visit a school in a neighborhood far away from your own, visit a Historically Black College or University (HBCU), or visit a church from a denomination other than your own, to learn more about these institutions and the essential role they have played in the development of Black excellence for more than a century.

Give face time to a greater variety of leaders. Schedule employees other than "the usual suspects" as speakers when you conduct all-hands or other employee events. Let employees see your talent bench so they understand that yours is not the only perspective influencing how the organization functions.

Prepare to answer the key REDI question. Giving yourself time to process your beliefs about REDI work is important. The most important thing is to make sure your personal beliefs do not intentionally or inadvertently derail the work.

So, please take the time to answer this question: **What words would you use to explain to an employee why you believe the organization should start or expand its REDI work?**

Step #5: Model the REDI way like the organization's primary change agent

Lawrence Hamilton is a former CHRO of Tech Data Corporation who advises executive teams about leadership strategy. He tells his clients that the most important way to make REDI real is to model the way. "Say what you mean, mean what you say, and consistently reinforce it by modeling the behavior or the outputs you want from other leaders," Lawrence advises.

Author and organizational consultant Ron Carucci says that nowadays leaders are being held to a higher standard of integrity than before. He noted that leadership honesty is being evaluated against three criteria: (1) Are you saying the right thing respectfully and directly (purpose)? (2) Are you doing the right and fair thing (justice)? and (3) Are you saying the right thing for the right reason (truth)? Employees and other stakeholders will test everything you do against this standard.

Your Get REDI prework will help you meet these standards, because if you know what you believe, you will be able to effectively model the way. And you will enhance your credibility with employees by incorporating purpose, justice, and truth into your REDI journey.

One note of caution: Driving change is not about driving people. As engineer-turned-change-evangelist April K. Mills would say, driving change requires you to "look for opportunities to influence the change, first by example and then by removing the obstacles that block others from also choosing the change." Driving change requires you to be ahead of those you lead. Your persistence in modeling the way is what will cause other leaders and managers to emulate the changes you are modeling! And that is how employees will see and feel the change.

EXECUTIVE SUMMARY

- Despite good intentions, some executives' REDI work may be hindered by implicit (unconscious) bias and by REDI anxieties.

- Leaders must recognize and fix their own implicit biases. However, REDI leadership success will depend more on addressing systemic bias in organizations than fixing individual employees' unconscious biases.

- Leaders who want to lead REDI strategy must intentionally learn about and connect with a wide range of employees.

- Use the five-step REDI Action model as a framework to prepare for modeling the way toward an inclusive organization.

- The essential executive mindset for driving REDI change is knowing your "why," and the essential behavior is modeling the way.

REDI QUESTIONS

How comfortable are you interacting with people who do not look like you? What can you do to enhance that comfort level? How can you set the expectation for employees in your company, especially those who manage others, that normal human variations such as race and ethnicity should not be used *against* candidates and employees? What is your organization doing to ensure the validity of the criteria your managers and HR professionals use to make talent decisions? What do you need to learn to enhance your impact as a change agent?

5

The Truth about Working in Your Organization

. . . .

The language of business is not the language of the soul or the language of humanity. It's a language of indifference; it's a language of separation, of secrecy, of hierarchy.
DAME ANITA RODDICK, in *The Corporation* by Joel Bakan

MY SECRET POWER is my ability to observe, understand, and influence individual and group human behavior in organizations. I identify what is working well and what is not, optimize and scale the good things, and minimize and eventually eliminate the less helpful ones. As an industrial/organizational psychologist and executive coach, my natural habitat is the workplace.

However, over my corporate life, two realities were constant frustrations. First, my executive clients seldom knew what was *really* going on in their organizations when it came to the human experience. Second, as I was dispensing advice based on years of education, experience, and applied research, I was usually having a poor experience myself. I had become adept at poker-facing my way through a series of disappointing jobs and had resigned myself to the idea that this is just how corporate life is: a bad deal that one tolerated. I seldom revealed my personal disappointments to my leaders, though, and I never let my clients know that I was experiencing many of the poor leadership behaviors that I was asking them to fix!

Those insights are why I confidently recommend that after the mindset check of the previous chapter, the next thing is getting a handle on what is *really* going on in your company. You probably do not know!

The Executive "Bubble" Is Soundproof

It is a truth, regularly discussed among employees, that the higher leaders are in organizations, the fewer details people share with you about what is happening below you. Management literature is replete with situations where critical information does not make it to the top of the organization in time to prevent a disaster. Similarly, the experience of employees from disadvantaged groups is getting attention for the first time, even though the sad realities were there all along. Was no one reporting them to top leaders? Had top leaders not created space for employees to tell these stories? Or had the leaders just not been listening when employees were trying to tell these stories?

I have worked with CEOs of some of the largest companies in the US and Canada. When I first began this work, I was surprised that, although executives wanted me in the room because of my technical expertise in organizational behavior, they were more excited when I shared stories from my conversations with people at other levels in the company or leaders in other companies. My clients loved those "not-available-elsewhere" insights because many CEOs live in a bubble, starving for insights about the goings-on below them. Sometimes it is easier to find out what is happening in your own company from external sources! Direct reports tend to parse and filter what they share for a variety of reasons. Sometimes they fear delivering bad news, or fear that what they share will make them look bad. Sometimes they are underinformed about what is happening in "their" part of the business, and about the issue at hand. The solution to this is partly within top leaders' control.

Psychological Safety and Good Ears

The higher you are in an organizational hierarchy, the harder you must work to encourage colleagues to tell you what is really happening below you. It isn't easy for employees to speak truth to power, so you must consistently and intentionally create conditions that will help employees speak up. Psychologist Amy Edmondson calls this "psychological safety": the confidence that candor and vulnerability are welcome. Psychological safety also means that when colleagues speak up, they should not have to worry about getting a negative response from you.

If psychological safety is present, the next critical precondition for getting "the scoop" is that you listen more than you tell. This is never easy, but when employees have a lot they want to say, the best thing to do is give them the microphone. According to recent research, corporations are starting to prioritize effective listening and other "social skills" more than ever when searching for new top executives.

Gorillas, Elephants, and Sieves!

Why else do executives miss out on the full story? In 1999, Dr. Daniel Simons ran a series of selective attention experiments in his experimental psychology lab. In the most famous of these, "Gorillas in Our Midst," Simons asked volunteers to count the number of times the people in a pre-recorded video threw a basketball to each other. Most study participants were so focused on counting the basketball passes that they did not notice the human in a gorilla suit who walked through the recorded scene! That research shows that "we think we see ourselves and the world as they really are, but we're actually missing a whole lot." Human perception can be inaccurate; we humans are often *unaware* of our mispercep-tions because, like implicit bias, our misperceptions are often *unconscious*. Make sure that your perceptions of employee experience are aligned with employees' realities!

Your understanding may also be obscured when others in the organization agree not to talk about what is really hap-pening. In his book *Rising to Power*, Ron Carucci discusses the concept of *mokita*, from the Kilivila language of Papua New Guinea. The word means something like "the truth we all know, but agree not to talk about," and it is akin to the American concept of "the elephant in the room." Unlike the invisible gorilla, the elephant in the room is about *conscious* decisions to avoid issues the group members perceive to be a psychological threat.

I was once part of a group where one highly energetic (and impulsive) person dominated each meeting by spout-ing ideas in rapid succession, leaving no room for others to have their say. The team leader would smile while this per-son spoke but never intervened. The result is that me and my eye-rolling colleagues believed he cared more about the inconsiderate bully's ideas than about ours. The elephant in the room was, "Why doesn't the leader shut this down and stop wasting our time?" No one ever told him he was losing his team's confidence, one overbearing meeting at a time. Be sure to make space for various perspectives so you can avoid repeating ineffective behaviors.

Additionally, colleagues may only tell you what they think you want you to hear. Another concept Ron and I discussed was "sifted data." Data are "sifted" when your advisors don't tell you "the whole story," leaving you with a distorted view of organizational reality. The story I shared in Chapter 3 about the CHRO who hid some employee survey insights from the CEO is an example of the sifted data phenomenon.

"Gorillas, elephants, and sieves" are cautions for any leader, particularly with REDI. After all, your typical day-to-day experiences likely differ from those of your employees, customers, and suppliers. Add to that the fact that employees may avoid telling you the truth or might tell you only what that they think you want to hear. And to top it off, because you are human, you might misperceive some things and fail to perceive others!

You can overcome these barriers by making it okay to speak up, by listening more than you tell, by asking incisive questions, and by making sure you get data from a variety of sources and do not over-rely on your inner circle.

Effective Leadership Is Not "Soft"

Many executives have the unfortunate habit of using the term "soft skills" when discussing the human experience in the workplace. I wish that term could be banned. "Soft" in this context implies that the human experience is less important than other core business concerns (hard skills). But what could be more core to business success than the experience of the employees who devise, create, market, sell, and deliver the company's products and services? Isn't the human experience *the* key ingredient in the recipe that defines the enterprise's secret sauce?

This unfortunate hierarchy, in which the human experience is ranked lower than other aspects of the work, may begin as early as when leaders get their college educations. US employers say that business students are not well versed in the interpersonal aspects of leadership, partially because "soft skills," though emphasized in liberal arts education, are underemphasized in business schools.

Dr. Thomas Kolditz and his colleagues at the Doerr Institute for New Leaders at Rice University concluded that the traditional model of leadership development promulgated by the nation's top business schools focuses on gaining knowledge and getting a degree but not enough on "how to become a certain kind of person." The kind of person he means is a purpose-driven leader who "never sees other people as merely an expedient means to one's own career success and who earns the trust and love of those they lead." A leader like this would not only have mastery of operational aspects of business but also of leading the human experience. A leader with this balanced perspective could drive innovation, customer experience, *and* REDI leadership. In response, the Carnegie Foundation is implementing a program to elevate leadership development across the nation.

It's Never Too Late to Address REDI

Framing the human experience at work as tangential to core business concerns may partially explain why some executives dodge conversations about race, ethnicity, gender, and other natural human variation in the workplace. These topics were not new to the executives I interviewed for this book, but all said they were more confident dealing with other aspects of their business than with REDI. Now that there is an increased expectation that they play a more prominent REDI role, leaders said they had not been trained to think of these issues as critical to their leadership effectiveness. No wonder they are tentative!

Tim Ryan, PwC's US chair and senior partner, offers the best advice about this: "Don't worry about saying the wrong thing... create an environment where you can have these conversations... It's okay not to have a perfect story."

Harvard Kennedy School lecturer in public policy Dr. Robert Livingston writes that "racial discrimination is prevalent in the workplace, and... organizations with strong commitments to diversity are no less likely to discriminate." And yet, he writes, "One senior executive told me, 'We don't have any discriminatory policies in our company.'" One of Livingston's main points is that leaders may be out of touch with the experiences of people from underrepresented groups and those who are described as "different" within their organizations and in the broader community. He noted that "too few of us believe that our leaders provide the psychologically safe spaces we would need to speak up." These ideas are borne out in the research nFormation published in 2022, showing that women of color are yearning for a new kind of workplace, reimagined to support authenticity and new forms of power.

People of color have
the same brain, just in a more
colorful wrapper, and your
organization may be missing
out on that potential benefit!

Executives cannot avoid dealing directly with REDI as a core leadership imperative. Black employees, and all employees who have been subordinated, need your emotional support. They need to know that you care about their day-to-day experiences at work and want those experiences to be positive. Mr. Floyd's death was an emotional turning point, not just for Black America, but for all of America. As business-woman and chairwoman of Starbucks Corporation Mellody Hobson says, this is "Civil Rights 3.0," a new day in which "the broader society is keeping score. There are consequences that exist for not living up to those commitments."

What Is Your Organization's Current State of REDI-ness?

David Lancefield and I noted that three primary challenges persist regarding the Black experience in corporate America. First, historically and currently, Black Americans are called back for interviews, and hired, at lower rates than other ethnic groups. Second, Black Americans are also promoted at lower rates than other race and ethnic groups. As a result, we are overrepresented in lower-level jobs and underrepresented in white-collar and leadership roles. Third, our day-to-day experiences at work are less positive than those of people from other races and ethnic groups. This last challenge is not a diversity issue; it is an issue of inclusion.

As business leaders begin to address REDI in the workplace, most direct their human resources departments to hire more people of color. However, since underrepresentation (diversity) and day-to-day experience (inclusion) are distinct issues, solutions must also be distinct. Your first remit as a senior leader is to clarify whether you have a diversity issue, an inclusion issue, both issues, an equity issue, or no issue at all. Let's start by defining the potential clues as to which challenge(s) might exist in your organization.

Diversity issue. You might have a diversity issue if the people of color in your organization are

- underrepresented at the point of entry into the organization; or

- missing from the ranks of your direct or plus-one reports and from the ranks of your professional analysts and advisors—in other words, if you can do your job as a leader without regularly interreacting with at least one person who is not from the *reference group* (the group that is larger, has more power, etc.), your organization probably lacks adequate diversity.

Inclusion issue. You might have an inclusion issue if

- you do not realize or believe that people of color have workplace experiences that differ from those of the reference group (usually White employees);

- you notice that the same people are mentioned for projects, and their voices are heard the loudest;

- there are few to no people of color in your business development and sales roles, roles that are external client-facing, or roles that generate the bulk of the revenue for your business and, therefore, have more influence in the organization—if that power is not being shared with a diverse group of employees; or

- there are few to no people of color in the parts of your organization that are empowered to create and enhance your products, such as product innovation, product management, and engineering. These are the roles that define the organization's future. Is that future being defined from only one perspective?

Diversity and inclusion issue. You might both have issues if any of the following are true:

- People of color in your organization do not speak up when they are invited to offer their opinions.

- You call people of color "minorities." That word is offensive because it explicitly defines one group as having power and the other group as subordinate to that power. It also implies that "minority" is a permanent state from which one cannot escape. Consider replacing that word with one that accurately describes the situation of the group to which you are referring, such as "underrepresented," "subordinated," or "marginalized."

- You have a strategy that treats Black people, Hispanic/Latino people, Asian Americans and Pacific Islanders, and Native Americans as "the minorities" and assumes these groups have one common experience. None of these groups is a monolith and, as I will show later, each has highly variable and unique experiences in US workplaces.

Equity issue. You might have an equity issue if

- you discover that employees of color are mostly hired and promoted into the lowest-paying, most onerous, and least flexible jobs that are at "the bottom of the list" in terms of desirability;

- employees of color are required to wait longer than other employees for promotions or other career mobility opportunities; or

- women of color are compensated significantly less than their colleagues even though they make the same contributions.

If you have these patterns of race- or ethnicity-based disparity in your organization, you have diversity, equity, and inclusion problems and talent-optimization problems. People of color have the same brain, just in a more colorful wrapper, and your organization may be missing out on that potential benefit!

Of course, you will need to focus on talent management and resource allocation processes and outcomes to really understand your organization's REDI-ness. Pay special attention to hiring, career mobility, and compensation.

To Understand Employee Experiences, Follow the Leader

I tell executive teams that to really understand employee experience, you must "follow the leader"! If leadership effectiveness scores are low in a part of the business (or the overall business), employee engagement, satisfaction, and retention will likely also be low. Decades of employee opinion data show that managers have the greatest impact on the day-to-day experience of employees.

Whether you have a REDI strategy or not, the first clue to understanding what is happening in your organization is how employees perceive their managers. On one hand, ineffective managers cannot engage or retain high-performing employees, nor do they support REDI outcomes. When employees do not feel welcome, they leave. On the other hand, managers who support the success of each team member, including those whose human variation is less common in the overall workforce, will have thriving teams that can attract and retain the best talent. I call this "100% Leadership."

So, what is a leader to do? You need a clear sense of the day-to-day experience of *all* your employees. And you need to make sure that your managers are inclusive. You need to set an immutable 100% Leadership expectation, even if that means you must ask your favorite colleague to leave the organization. I'll address this Boldness aspect of the Inclusion MBA model in the next few chapters.

EXECUTIVE SUMMARY

- Executives exist in a "bubble" that may obscure certain realities of employee experience.

- You must create a culture of psychological safety and then listen intently to what employees want to share.

- To really understand employee experience, understand how managers behave.

- Insist that managers support *all* employees (not just the chosen few) with 100% Leadership.

REDI QUESTIONS

Do you feel you have a good sense of the goings-on in your organization from the employees' perspective? In which areas do you have doubts? Do you ever sense that your direct reports are not telling you everything you need to hear? What can you do to make it clear that you want to hear the unvarnished truth? What behaviors would you need to start, stop, or change to create an environment in which the organization's top leaders and other employees will tell you the whole story? Are your managers 100% Leaders?

PART THREE

BOLDNESS

MAKE INCLUSION
SCALABLE

Inclusion Reframe #2: Boldness

*I will be thoughtful and careful about who I empower
to lead the humans in this organization!*

6

CEO and Board
Using the Same Playbook

. . . .

*I cannot think of a single case of radical change that has
taken place at a large organization without the support of top
leaders—whether it was a CEO, a board member, or both.*

DR. ROBERT LIVINGSTON, *The Conversation*

JUDGING FROM the hesitancy I observed in many
CEOs' initial responses to calls for corporate leadership on social justice issues, I wondered how corporate boards were supporting them in speaking about
the subject. So, I attended the 2020 annual summit of the
National Association of Corporate Directors (NACD) to learn
more. NACD is the nation's premier non-profit organization
for educating corporate board directors, so this was an ideal
place to read the pulse of corporate board leaders. I settled in
for what I expected to be a few days of routine talk about corporate governance, but NACD 2020 surprised me in a few ways.

The summit began with a thunderous bang, with a chat
about capitalism and philanthropy between author Anand
Giridharadas and Columbia Business School Dean Emeritus

R. Glenn Hubbard. Giridharadas, known for his regular take-no-prisoners skewering of the financial "elite," has a brand I would describe as an "edgy gadfly." Conversely, Hubbard, a former chairman of the Council of Economic Advisers under President George W. Bush, is staid and traditional. So, this was bound to be a battle of wits, social class, economic policy, *and* style.

Unsurprisingly, Giridharadas pulled no punches and ruffled many when, early in the conversation, he asked, "Where were you in the run-up to the climate crisis? Where were you during widening inequality over the last four decades? Where were you in the run-up to the subprime crisis? Where were you in the run-up to the opioid crisis? Where were you?"

His point was that the current social realities should not be surprising to corporate directors. He argued that the social and economic factors that led to disparate outcomes from the pandemic had been building for decades. He intimated that board directors had the power and money to influence these outcomes positively, but had not done so because it was not in their economic self-interest. Sure, Giridharadas was over the top, but that is his "thing." His comments that day were true to form and in no way surprising to anyone who follows his work.

But some board members demanded refunds and threatened to quit the NACD in protest. In response, NACD CEO Peter Gleason made a statement in the press that included this quote: "Key to NACD's mission, especially at our annual NACD Summit, is to expose our 21,000 members to contrasting views on the issues that will redefine how businesses create value." That was a courageous response, considering that many summit participants seemed unaccustomed and resistant to "contrasting views." It raised the question, "Why do some corporate directors respond with such defensiveness when exposed to unfamiliar or challenging ideas?" I wondered how those directors react when CEOs come to them with REDI proposals, which fall squarely into the "unfamiliar and challenging" category.

This opening conversation and the NACD response were pleasant surprises. I saw many other signs that NACD members were paying attention to REDI matters, including that several mainstage and expert sessions explicitly addressed REDI issues.

NACD 2020 was clearly on a mission to help participants become more informed and activated about REDI, and board directors were becoming informed. Although some thought the subject was irrelevant to shareholder returns, many wanted to know more. Once board directors know more, I believe they will offer more full-throated support for REDI work.

CEO and Board Tackling Inclusion Strategy

In her 2021 book *How Boards Work*, economist Dr. Dambisa Moyo notes that "corporate boards exist to help senior management" target opportunities and confront challenges. She writes that the board's primary role is to help senior management set the strategy for the organization so it can function well and generate positive returns. A board, she says, is also responsible for being "vigilant" about external shocks. Moyo calls out racial inequality as an urgent problem, and she calls for CEOs and other senior leaders to take ownership of REDI risks. Note: Moyo was a member of the UK's Commission on Race and Ethnic Disparities (CRED), which concluded, in 2021, that Britain is no longer a country "where the system is deliberately rigged against ethnic minorities." Many academicians and social justice activists challenged several of the CRED conclusions and recommendations. My parents were part of the generation of West Indians who went to the UK in the 1950s to help rebuild after the Blitz, and I was born there. My many relatives and friends said the CRED conclusions did not align with their day-to-day experiences.

Nevertheless, Moyo's book is great, and she makes it clear that times are a-changing when it comes to REDI. She even points out that Warren Buffett's stance that social change should be led by governments and not corporations may be out of sync with the zeitgeist. Moreover, she notes that this shifting landscape is heavily influenced by institutional investors' attention to ESG issues—the umbrella under which some boards are now classifying REDI issues.

So, let's move ahead with the assumption that boards know they have a critical role in guiding senior management to effective enterprise-wide REDI strategies. But, even with that assumption, some corporate leaders have told me they still do not have full-throated board support for REDI work, usually for one of these reasons:

1 **Taboo.** In some cases, conversations about "race" are taboo within the board and organizational cultures.

2 **Culture.** The board and the organization's culture may not support the conversations, actions, and pace of change needed to produce meaningful REDI strategies.

3 **Relationships.** As David Fubini so clearly points out, "The CEO's relationship with their board is almost always challenging, at times taxing, often contentious, and always

Progress on REDI will be influenced
by how board directors interact
among themselves and with the CEO
and by the organization's pattern
of responding to change.

requires constant attention." Suppose the CEO's relationship with the board is not strong. In that case it will be challenging to get support for a powerful REDI strategy that can be implemented apace and produce meaningful results.

4   **Definitions.** Some boards need to develop a shared understanding of what "diversity and inclusion" outcomes are meaningful for their organization. REDI strategy always requires bespoke solutions, so board and management alignment is essential.

5   **Stakeholders.** Boards have traditionally focused on shareholder profit as their primary measure of organizational success. Now, some are grappling with the stakeholder-primacy model, in which stakeholder-employees would have more influence. Of course, this model is not the future, it is already here, but some board directors still need to be nudged into embracing the idea.

6   **Lack of diversity.** The boards of most US companies are not diverse. As a result, many board directors may not have a realistic view of the experience of their employees of color. It is hard for a company to have a diverse and inclusive workforce if the board is not diverse and does not understand the concerns of people of color!

7   **The business case.** Boards (and CEOs) have typically discussed REDI issues within a "business case" framework that focuses on its value for driving profitability or other financial outcomes. However, boards need to pivot to focus on employee experience and customer expectations to help point the CEO to a meaningful REDI strategy.

8   **REDI Mindset.** All board members must, as individuals, search their conscience about their REDI Mindset. Even if a board director does not believe that REDI issues deserve prominence among their other priorities, they will need to subordinate those opinions to the common good and the zeitgeist; the horse is (finally) out of the barn when it comes to REDI matters. An organization led by a REDI-recalcitrant board will likely quickly lose ground to its competitors.

Ultimately, board members must overcome the forces constraining corporate America's REDI action.

Overcome "race" as a taboo subject

Many corporate leaders approach REDI with kid gloves. Some might even say that it is still taboo to talk about race in America generally, particularly in business settings. As recently as 2009, psychoanalyst Dr. Gwen Bergner wrote an entire book, entitled *Taboo Subjects: Race, Sex, and Psychoanalysis*, to teach her psychology colleagues how to become more proficient and "comfortable" in dealing with race. After all, the social hierarchies we take for granted define our development and affect our overall lives. Psychologists and psychiatrists, whose work helps us become psychologically healthier, must know how to talk about race if they are to be deemed competent to counsel *all* clients. It is the same for corporate directors: your workforce, clientele, and communities are diverse, and investors believe REDI competency is necessary for your success. It is impossible to effectively lead a diverse group of stakeholders if you do not understand the various perspectives they represent.

Therefore, both CEOs and boards must get comfortable talking about race and ethnicity. You can't generate realistic solutions to challenges that have their basis in race if you can't even talk about the subject. Encourage your board to do the following:

1   Ask questions about the current state of REDI in your organization. Part of the board's fiduciary responsibility is to understand the workforce diversity and inclusion patterns and support strategies that enable all employees to thrive.

2   Invite people who represent the range of human variation to be part of the board.

3   Include employees on your board of directors as another way to enhance the alignment between corporate board decision making and employee experience. Employee participation also makes partnership and shared understanding between boards and employees explicit. This practice is not commonplace in US companies, and the impact of worker board participation on company financial performance is unclear. However, as previously discussed, shareholder value should not be the sole measure of company performance anyway. Including employees on corporate boards could reduce corporate missteps regarding overall employee experience, specifically regarding REDI.

4   Work with an inclusion coach so that individual board members and the overall board understand how employees will interpret their behavior and REDI strategies. A coach can also help board members develop multicultural competence and build relationships with people who seem "different" or unfamiliar.

5   Take a leadership stance on REDI matters, empowering the CEO to do the same.

6   Read the recommended resources for this chapter in the Further Reading section of this book.

Overcome a REDI-averse culture

I define culture as what it feels like to work in an organization (or on a board) and do business with the organization. Workplace cultures are shared, pervasive, enduring, and implicit and impact most interpersonal and group outcomes. Board culture (the way the board interacts and makes decisions) affects the board's guidance to the CEO, and as we all know, that guidance significantly influences CEO action (or inaction).

Harvard professor Dr. Boris Groysberg and his colleagues created the Integrated Culture Framework that might help you think about how your board's culture and the larger organization interact. Culture is mapped along two dimensions in this model—how people interact and how they respond to change—and different culture styles can be identified on the resulting matrix. Of course, there are pros and cons to each style. Still, the *caring culture*, in which the work environment (board, C-suite, overall organization) is warm, sincere, and relational, is the style that supports teamwork, engagement, communication, trust, and belonging. A board culture like this is also necessary to support progress on REDI. Do a quick assessment of the current board culture, especially if you are a joint chair/CEO, to determine if it can effectively support the changes necessary to define and implement a REDI strategy. Any enhancements to board culture will also enhance your success in leading other critical organizational changes.

Overcome a REDI-hesitant board

Of course CEOs should have positive relationships with board directors. However, these relationships can vary significantly, which can affect the design and success of the

The emotional component
of this work and the vulnerability it
requires might be an opportunity
for CEOs and board members.
It could connect them and enhance
their shared REDI understanding.

REDI strategy. The CEO is also the board chair in about 67 percent of large US public companies, according to Dr. Dambisa Moyo. Private and smaller companies are more likely to use an independent lead director model, and according to the NACD, that role is rising. Regardless of the governance structure, the board and the CEO must be active partners in defining REDI strategy.

Since this topic needs to permeate all aspects of your business operation, the CEO and the board should have what David Fubini calls an "unobstructed view" of the REDI strategy. It is not enough for the CEO, the CDO, and the rest of the C-suite to develop a strategy and then sell it to the board. Given the unfamiliarity and visibility of the subject, directors are likely to interrogate any REDI strategy. And the board may need the CEO to provide more hand-holding and reassurance than is typical, because REDI work has a more significant emotional component than many other urgent issues.

The emotional component of this work and the vulnerability it requires might be an opportunity for CEOs and board members. It could connect them in new ways and enhance their shared understanding of not just REDI but other employee-centered outcomes. As defined in Chapter 1, "diversity" is about counting the numbers of people of color, while "inclusion" is about building organizational cultures that value those people of color, enabling them to be seen, heard, and recognized and their talents to be optimized. However, the terms "diversity" and "inclusion" mean different things to different people. As part of your REDI journey, define what those terms mean to you, what goals you want to set regarding diversity and inclusion, and how you will measure progress.

You also want to decide which aspects of human variation you will focus on in this work. There are a few ways to think about this. For example, you might choose to focus on the characteristics protected by US federal law: race, color, religion, sex (including pregnancy, sexual orientation, and gender identity), national origin, age, disability, and genetic information. You will also want to look at the various ways these characteristics intersect with one another. For example, women feel less valued, less recognized, and less like they belong than men, and Black women consistently report the lowest belonging scores among all women. Additionally, relative to all women, most Black women have never interacted with a senior leader in their organization! It is essential to tease out these nuances.

You might also consider additional demographic dimensions along which the employee and applicant experience might vary and include them in your exploration. For example, people from subordinated groups are often underrepresented in management, external client-facing roles, product development and innovation, and other high-visibility roles. Or, if you operate a global business from US headquarters, employees outside the US may feel less supported than their US colleagues. As I said at the beginning, I focused this book primarily on race- and ethnicity-based REDI, but I hope you realize that you can apply these ideas to support interrogating any human variations that are meaningful for your organization.

Overcome lack of diversity on the board itself

The Alliance for Board Diversity, in collaboration with Deloitte, published its sixth edition of the *Missing Pieces* report in June 2021. The report analyzed Fortune 500 board composition by race, gender, and ethnicity, revealing the patterns we are all working to change. For example, Hispanics/

Latinos (19 percent of the population, but 4 percent of board seats) and Black Americans (13 percent of the population but 9 percent of board seats) are underrepresented on boards. Asian Americans and Pacific Islanders (AAPI) hold 5 percent of board seats (but are 6 percent of the population). Native American or Native Alaskan representation in corporate leadership is so low that they disappear when US labor force data is disaggregated!

The S&P 500 is making inroads. The most recent Spencer Stuart report, analyzed in the *Wall Street Journal*, showed that from May 2020 to May 2021, the companies that make up the S&P 500 "sharply increased" the number of new Black and Latino directors on their boards. According to the report, about 11 percent of all directors on S&P 500 boards are Black, 30 percent are women, 4 percent are Hispanic/Latino, and 6 percent are AAPI. Less than 1 percent are Native American or Native Alaskan (Native Americans and Native Alaskans are about 3 percent of the population), and less than 1 percent belong to multiple racial groups.

Corporate board diversity is relevant to this REDI conversation because, as Russell Reynolds Associates eloquently stated in their *Different Is Better* report, executives' and board directors' experiences, demographic characteristics, and personal characteristics influence their perspectives. Drs. Steven Creek, Kristine Kuhn, and Arvin Sahaym's research shows that firms with diverse boards are more likely to adopt programs that "signal organizational support for employees and benevolence, and these programs foster more positive satisfaction levels." In other words, more diverse boards are more likely to support progressive management programs, and those programs have a positive effect on day-to-day employee experience.

When I started to conceptualize this book, I could think of no one better than Shellye Archambeau, former CEO of MetricStream and board member of Verizon, Roper, and Okta, to discuss ideas about the strategic implementation of REDI work. I interviewed her in November of 2020, a month after the publication of her compelling book *Unapologetically Ambitious* and a month before *Fortune* magazine selected it as one of their top business books of 2020. In her uniquely unambiguous way, Shellye offered several tips, many of which I have incorporated in various chapters of this book. For example, here is what she told me about the importance of diversity in leadership: "Women and Black women should be everywhere because we have a perspective to offer that needs to be included when leaders make decisions. The best teams represent a wide variety of perspectives and experience and get the best results the first time, with fewer unforced errors."

Nasdaq has implemented its own "Inclusive Entrepreneurship" framework as a way to address "deep social disparities that undermine the growth and potential of entrepreneurs of color." Additionally, Deloitte and the NACD have defined a Board Inclusion Framework. These two frameworks will be helpful in your assessment of the maturity of your board's diversity as you set yourself up for success in defining and implementing your REDI strategy.

Overcome a business case focus above all else

Over my many years of consulting, leaders often asked about a "business case for diversity." Is it any wonder that I concluded that the denial and avoidance of REDI issues I regularly observed were focused, inappropriately, on money? Executives seldom mentioned anything else as often! I now have a stock response to any leader who asks me about the business case for REDI:

You can ask me for the business case if you want to know how I determined my consulting fee, but do not ask me about the business case if we are talking about enhancing the experience of people of color at work. That question suggests people of color must "pay to play," that you will only treat us fairly and equitably if we can show you that there is a financial payoff to doing so.

That is a pull-no-punches response that, I think, gets to the heart of that matter.

This "business case" framing is so commonplace that I expect it comes up whenever executives discuss REDI issues with board directors. I read a *Wall Street Journal* opinion piece by Arthur Levitt Jr., former chair of the Securities and Exchange Commission (SEC), in January 2021. The article, "If Corporate Diversity Works, Show Me the Money," was not meant so much to display antipathy to REDI work as to showcase his investor-above-all-else view of corporate priorities. I realized that (1) he had so clearly expressed his point of view that I could use it to build teaching points to refute the "profit-above-all-else" approach to REDI, and (2) many board directors and executives might agree with his ideas. So, I want to equip you with the counterpoints from the perspective of a person of color who perceives these ideas as *offensive, oppressive, and obstructive.* Employees who are subordinated and waiting for systemic change know that disproportionately focusing on "the money" only perpetuates the very problem that needs to be solved.

The *Journal* published Levitt's opinion piece in response to Nasdaq's December 2020 proposal that its listed companies appoint at least one woman and one person from an underrepresented racial, ethnic, or LGBTQ+ group to their boards of directors. (As mentioned earlier, a slightly modified version of Nasdaq's proposal won SEC approval in August 2021.) Levitt's commentary addressed that proposal but also provided details about a mindset that can be counterproductive to corporate and board progress on REDI.

- Levitt argued that diversity requirements are political; he seemed to mean that in the literal sense of Democrats versus Republicans.

My counter: Employees of color have less than ideal experiences in corporations every day. That's why we have such strong opinions about REDI and why we expect better from our leaders. "Diversity requirements" are a matter of whether we will be allowed to thrive or not. We interpret the requirement for a REDI "business case" to mean you want us to pay to play. Yet, you don't ask others to justify their hiring, even when they make it into the candidate pool on the basis of networks or other less-than-"meritocratic" criteria. That's a double standard, and we feel this way regardless of how we vote.

- The opinion piece also suggested that diversity on boards is emotional, and often "creates more heat than light."

My counter: It may indeed be necessary to have some "heat" in the boardroom. Employees of color experience that heat every day, but we don't have a way to turn it off or avoid it. If REDI concerns are emotional for boards, imagine how challenging they are for people of color every day!

- Levitt further argued that data do not demonstrate a clear link between racial and ethnic diversity and "actual performance."

Employees who are subordinated
and waiting for systemic change
know that disproportionately
focusing on "the money" only
perpetuates the very problem
that needs to be solved.

My counter: In the years this business case approach has been championed, researchers have definitely documented the benefits businesses derive from workforce diversity. Diversity offers a variety of advantages, regardless of the aspect of human variation you are analyzing. For example, in an *American Sociological Review* article published in 2009, Dr. Cedric Herring found that "racial diversity is associated with increased sales revenue, more customers, greater market share, and greater relative profits." Gender diversity, he found, is similarly associated with increased sales revenue, more customers, and greater relative profits. Organizations derive positive outcomes when the workforce is neurodiverse and LGBTQ+-supportive.

The fact is that the known positive outcomes of workplace diversity have never been enough to enhance leader action on REDI. Workplace diversity has also been proven to positively affect business outcomes, including profits, innovation, and decision making. Diversity can also enhance corporate board performance. Nevertheless, that proven "business case for diversity" has not resulted in a rush to demographic diversification in corporations.

- He also argued that if racial and ethnic diversity were financially good for companies, they would already be doing it.

My counter: This point is so offensive that I respond to it only for the sake of thoroughness. First, it implies that racial and ethnic diversity is an optional feature of corporate governance. I have argued the opposite: REDI issues are essential, and they should be central to the leadership strategy of the enterprise. Second, this point assumes the companies not "doing it" are acting rationally. Companies that are not doing it may think that subordinating a portion of their workforce is rational, but a financial measure of diversity is only reasonable to those with the money, not those without it! And why would anyone celebrate resistance to diversity?!

Overcome "we're not REDI" mindsets

CEOs could be ahead of boards in your desire to influence inclusion strategy directly (leading), you could be behind the board (lagging), or you and the board could be in sync (aligned). The work you did to figure out your mindset with the REDI Skin in the Game Warm-Up is relevant here. Knowing more about where you stand on these problems, you can likely also see that the issues are highly emotional and that others' opinions are likely to be cemented. It might be helpful for your board members to do the same kind of self-exploration. Consider sharing the REDI Skin in the Game Warm-Up with them. You might also use a facilitator to manage a discussion about these topics professionally, helping leaders to talk about one of the most taboo topics in American business.

EXECUTIVE SUMMARY

- REDI strategy should be on the board's priority list.

- Boards must work intentionally to overcome the perceived and real hindrances to their REDI work.

- Diverse boards are needed to help drive REDI outcomes.

- The arguments against a leadership focus on REDI do not stand up to scrutiny.

- Individual board members must be willing to search their hearts if they are to make REDI progress. (Have them do the REDI Skin in the Game Warm-Up as a start.)

REDI QUESTIONS

What is your relationship like with your board? Is it collaborative or combative? Do your board members sincerely support REDI work, or are they just paying it lip service? Either way, what actions or behaviors tell you this is so? What would have to change for the board to fully support REDI work?

7

The C-Suite Inclusion Infusion

. . . .

Remember, people will judge you by
your actions, not your intentions.
You may have a heart of gold, but
so does a hard-boiled egg.
ATTRIBUTED TO MAYA ANGELOU

ONE OF MY executive coaching clients, a founding CEO in a start-up business, decided in June 2020 to "do something" to make sure all his employees were thriving. This exploration revealed great dissatisfaction in many business segments, especially among women and employees of color. The sales function, led by Pat, had lower employee survey scores than other teams.

Pat was one of the founders' buddies and one of the first employees hired. He worked hard, understood the work processes better than most, and was a stalwart advocate for the company. But Pat did not have an instinct for people leadership and was not trained as a professional leader. He threw tasks "over the wall" to his team with little guidance about the goal or how he would measure success. Pat also used a blue jay leadership style: he would bring a problem to the team, hover while asking for their solutions, and then hop out again to share those ideas with his peers as if they were his own. Pat did not go back to let his team know how he used their input, and he never gave them credit when he implemented their ideas. Pat also over-relied upon the opinions of a small group of close work buddies and did not advocate for the women on his team. Most people he managed perceived Pat to be an amiable but ineffective leader.

And then Pat did something that frustrated the CEO so much it changed their entire relationship. Pat sabotaged the organization's REDI work in his function. How did my client know that Pat was sabotaging the work? Simple—he watched Pat's actions:

- Pat gave the REDI ideas lip service when meeting with other executives but stonewalled and slow-walked every REDI action the leadership team agreed to implement. He also missed all the target dates for the REDI steps the CEO requested.

- Pat delegated key REDI responsibilities to someone else on his team but did not follow up to make sure they executed his instructions.

- When Pat announced the organization's REDI strategy to his management team, he used noncommittal language like, "This is what the executive team asked me to do"; "If you have any questions about why we are doing this, ask HR"; and "I know this is an additional ask, so I understand that you can't let it get in the way of your other priorities."

- Pat did not share the strategic business reasons for the REDI plans with his managers. As a result, lacking the "why," they could not cascade the strategy effectively.

Employees could see that Pat did not want to get with the REDI program. Eventually, the CEO came to grips with that reality too. He gave Pat an ultimatum: either support the work or leave the organization. Pat left. His personal beliefs did not support REDI work.

Your executive team members can make or break your efforts to build an inclusive culture. Some leaders will immediately see the need for this work and will do all they can to move it forward. I call these people the **REDI-mades**. Many will have mixed feelings. They might say, "You're giving me one more thing to worry about," or "Why do we have to rile people up?" I call these people the **Kinda-REDIs**. The third group comprises those who don't support this work at all. Whether this resistance is kept secret or expressed overtly, they are not likely to be advocates or champions. I call these people the **Not-REDIs**. You need a plan for all three possible REDI responses. Let the REDI-mades help you share your mission. Continuously show the Kinda-REDIs the data and personal feelings driving your REDI stance. And educate and monitor the Not-REDIs, making it clear that this work is an essential part of their jobs.

You must hold all executives accountable for getting REDI results, as if even one executive team member is not on board with your REDI efforts, you will not make significant progress.

Not-REDI reluctance stems from various sources, including deep-seated political and religious beliefs. Based on sentiment in the general population, we can anticipate that as many as 50 percent of leaders and managers might not naturally support REDI matters. Other Not-REDIs might fear being outed for failing to create engaging team cultures on teams they lead. Some Not-REDIs may lead parts of your business that lack diversity but may not want to change the

Your executive
team members can
make or break your
efforts to build an
inclusive culture.

way they work because the status quo has worked for them. For example, people of color tend to be underrepresented in sales and other external client-facing and revenue-generating roles in financial and professional services. You need to anticipate and understand those patterns (which I will explain in more detail later), so you know what is "typical" and what is an aberration. Of course, you should honor and respect leaders' personal beliefs and fears, but you must still insist that all leaders follow through on the actions that are part of their leadership obligations. You should clearly state your expectations and then hold all leaders, including the Not-REDIs, accountable for demonstrating the behaviors that match those expectations. You should anticipate that C-suite members' responses will vary and that there might be a pattern to that variation, sometimes based on the area of the business that person leads. And make sure you understand where each executive team member stands on REDI and *why* they have that stance. You will have to manage this variation effectively to get meaningful enterprise REDI outcomes.

Your work on the REDI Skin in the Game Warm-Up is relevant here. When you know where you stand on these issues, you are better prepared for the highly emotional nature of responses to REDI and understand that opinions are likely to be well cemented. Encourage your executive team and other leaders to do the same kind of self-exploration, even sharing the REDI Skin in the Game Warm-Up with them.

You might also use a facilitator to professionally manage a REDI discussion with you, the C-suite, and other top leaders about these topics. Do all you can to encourage leaders to talk about REDI issues so they become commonplace rather than taboo.

REDI Variations by Department

The guidance I am about to share comes from years of working with employee data (surveys, focus groups, operational data) from global companies. When the data are cut by functions, some consistent patterns emerge.

Each of the functions typically found in US corporations tends to have explicit and implicit ways of operating that yield unique REDI patterns. Functional units and departments have unique roles and power dynamics within their groups and as they interact with other functional units and departments in the organization. Organizations typically organize into *line functions* (which operate the business) and *staff functions* (which support the line in operating the business), setting up what professor Dr. Robert Golembiewski called the Neutral and Inferior Instrument model. The power differential between the line and staff roles creates tension and conflict.

Many leaders, including the legendary GE CEO Jack Welch, have sought out alternative organizational structures to this line/staff arrangement. In his 1990 annual report, Welch called for a "boundaryless company" that "would remove barriers among traditional functions, 'recognize no distinctions' between domestic and foreign operations, and 'ignore or erase group labels such as 'management,' 'salaried,' or 'hourly,' which get in the way of people working together."

Although many organizations, especially start-ups, have tried alternative leadership structures, the top-down, line/staff, boss/underling, salaried/hourly, and client-facing/non-client-facing distinctions persist. These organizational structures and power dynamics profoundly influence who gets which jobs, who gets promoted, and who is in the inner circle (or not) and, therefore, profoundly impact REDI outcomes.

US Bureau of Labor Statistics (BLS) data show that people of color are underrepresented in corporate roles and functions that wield significant direct power or decision-making and revenue-generating authority. These roles include senior leadership and management, marketing and sales managers, software developers, legal, and engineering. That BLS data show that Black Americans comprise 42.4 percent of mail sorters and 37.2 percent of nursing aides, but only 7.8 percent of management occupations and 4.1 percent of chief executives.

Since power and influence are the currency of organizational life, these influential roles are highly valued. Eventually they become commodities; available to those who know what buttons to push for access. Those who look most like the power holders go to the front of the line. Gatekeepers don't share the "code," intentionally keeping the inner circle small and exclusive. Over time, these powerful functions become more demographically homogenous.

REDI Variations by Class

Columbia professor Dr. Paul Ingram notes that "people with higher origins cluster in high-status departments; those with lower origins work in less-visible groups. Because companies often seek candidates for managerial roles from only a handful of departments, the odds are stacked against some of the best candidates simply because they work in the wrong place."

Additionally, some employees of color, and people of any race whose social and economic circumstances constrain their social mobility, encounter barriers to career access. For example:

- Corporations tend to develop patterns of recruiting from specific colleges and universities, especially for high-profile, client-facing roles, which effectively excludes those from other schools from those plum jobs.

- Higher education in the US is currently structured such that the students who have greater access to it and to the so-called "best" colleges and universities are the same students who already have other advantages (like social networks and financial flexibility) that propel their careers. The *New York Times* reports that "even though most lower-income students fare well at elite colleges, there are relatively few of them there." Attending the "best" universities confers not just a high-quality education but lifelong access to social networks. Conversely, lack of access to these institutions constrains career progression for those who lack that pedigree.

- Corporations might not recruit from the schools attended by people of color, even though schools that educate students from "modest" backgrounds are more successful at "pushing those students into the middle class" than the so-called "elite" schools.

- Unless a guidance counselor or other interested party shares information about the job opportunities available in corporations, students from less advantaged backgrounds might be unaware of those options, and access to them might seem out of the realm of possibility. If students have never known anyone who held such a job, they might not seek one out.

- Potential hires may not have equal access to technical tools to apply for the jobs, develop skills for the jobs, or the ability to work from home (if the job allows for or requires that). This is the digital divide that became clearer and was exacerbated by the COVID-19 pandemic.

- Some potential hires will not have the financial resources for extended childcare beyond the school day to allow for after-hours hobnobbing that facilitates the relationship-building that is so valued in corporate life. Women and other caregivers are often forced to make choices that can reduce their social currency, even if they wish they could do otherwise.

- Some leaders may exclude employees who do not look like them because their speech, dress, hairstyles, and interaction patterns are unfamiliar.

All these factors can significantly influence a person's long-term career prospects. Leaders of the business areas that have disproportionate power and influence may already be aware of the national statistics, power patterns, and career mobility challenges mentioned above. However, they may not have considered how these dynamics relate to REDI outcomes. Challenge them to (1) know and be able to explain the nuances of the workforce composition in their departments; (2) develop hypotheses about what actions might be needed to address and redress any observed disparities in their teams; (3) create and implement plans to seek regular feedback from their teams, so they can understand all employees' day-to-day experiences; and (4) specify outcomes, with clearly defined success criteria, for improving any disparities.

Build a High-Level REDI
Strategy before You Hire a CDO

Once you and your executive team have started the REDI conversation, you or your Chief Human Resources Officer might be tempted to hire a head of diversity and inclusion or Chief Diversity Officer, to whom you could delegate the responsibility for building the REDI strategy. You would not be the only one. CDO and DE&I leader hiring increased dramatically between 2020 and 2021; more than sixty US companies hired their first-ever CDO.

The work that is now generally called "diversity and inclusion" is relatively new; most started only in the 1960s in response to the Civil Rights movement. Initially, the focus was training managers to avoid the legal risks that could come from violating federal civil rights laws. Over time, the focus has broadened to include strategically building psychologically healthy workplaces, product design and customer intimacy, and training in multicultural competency and unconscious bias awareness. Today many large US companies have a CDO, the top executive job responsible for REDI strategy across the organization. The CDO typically reports directly to the CEO, not the CHRO, and likely has a voice in the enterprise conversation not just about talent, but also about product and service design and delivery. If you are leading a smaller organization, you might not have a CDO, and this work might fall under the umbrella of your CHRO or head of human resources.

The executive team should develop a shared understanding of the initial points of focus for REDI work before you hire a new CDO or start large-scale REDI work. Don't hire a CDO until you have a good a sense of what really matters.

Don't hire a CDO and
set them up to waste time
wrangling the C-suite
to determine their mandate.
Define the mandate first.

Not only would that CDO be operating without the necessary strategic guidance, but you might rein them in just when they start gaining momentum. David Lancefield would say that trying to change a culture, for example, to one that values inclusion requires a clear, compelling strategic direction. Otherwise, you will be wasting your effort and may create unintended disruption. Don't hire a CDO and set them up to waste time wrangling the C-suite to determine their mandate. Define the mandate first.

Create Your REDI Vision

Now that you have thought about your mindset, as well as the mindset of your board and executive team, you are a little closer to guiding the rest of the organization in defining that REDI mandate. Your HR leaders and others will likely have already started ad hoc efforts to get the ball rolling on REDI work. Diversity and inclusion practitioners often say, "There is so much to do," meaning they can't wait for every strategic "i" to be dotted before they act. You shouldn't necessarily curtail those efforts. However, those same practitioners could accomplish so much more with the wind of your strategic guidance at their backs.

If you create a high-level REDI Vision *before* you select a CDO, the person you hire will have the clarity needed to hit the ground running. Use the six-point REDI Vision framework below to organize your thoughts. At the end of this list, I have provided a handy worksheet that you and all executive team members can use to help you create your REDI Vision.

Note: You can also download the REDI Vision materials at leadinginclusion.com.

Action #1: Assess

Assess the current organizational culture and employee experience. Your team can accomplish this by using employee surveys, reviewing passive operational and performance data, and conducting interviews and focus groups.

Action #2: Define your REDI BHAG

What is your Big Hairy Audacious Goal (BHAG) when it comes to REDI? It should be a North Star, not a detailed strategy, and should answer questions like, "What do you want to accomplish?" (beyond, for example, simply "diverse representation"); "What do you want employees (and other stakeholders) to say about REDI twelve months from now?" and "What matters for *your* organization?" For example, your BHAG could be, "In the next twelve months, I want our company to be on *Fortune* magazine's list of top companies on diversity and inclusion." The BHAG doesn't state exactly how it will be accomplished; it sets an aspirational and understandable target. Think as well about how the CDO (or other team members to whom you assign this work) will need to support that BHAG within your organizational structure.

Action #3: Make REDI work core work

In our interview, Shellye Archambeau said, "Anything that's not core to the strategy does not get done. If you want to see improvements in diversity and inclusion outcomes, make the work part of the overall business strategy." Think about how REDI might enhance the success of your current business strategy and if or how the existing strategy might need to be tweaked to incorporate a REDI perspective.

Involve the entire C-suite
in defining the REDI Vision
and hold them accountable
for outcomes that support
your REDI Vision.

Action #4: Define the focus

Define the specific REDI elements on which you want the organization to focus. Respect? Equity? Diversity? Inclusion? Some or all? Refer to the definitions in Chapter 1 if you need a refresher on the differences between the aspects of REDI.

One myth I can dispel is that your jobs are so exotic that people of diverse backgrounds will not have the skills to fill them. As Andrea Hoffman, diversity strategist and founder and CEO of Culture Shift Labs, said in an interview with me, "Don't ever say the phrase, 'We can't find any [talent from underrepresented groups]!' That's not true and it'll never be true. If you're still thinking or saying that, it means you are not trying hard enough or that you're going about it the wrong way. The first question you should ask is, 'What is the right way to achieve this goal?' and then, 'How can we do it at an accelerated pace?' You must set a target, share it with your team, empower them to come up with the right ideas, get out of their way, and say yes to the solutions they present. And tie leader bonuses to these outcomes."

Shellye Archambeau remarked, "If you want a diverse organization, you need to ask, 'What is a reasonable target based upon the number of people we hire in a given year?' Then establish and communicate the targets. Keep working toward your targets and be transparent with your organization. When you make progress, celebrate, and when you fail, recommit to even more work. You don't give up and you don't hide either. The issue is, there's a lack of development, there's a lack of sponsorship, there's a lack of opportunity. There's a lack of risk taking. And there's a lack of intention. But there is definitely not a lack of talent."

Will your REDI Vision focus only on talent and HR issues or also on product and service issues? On supply chain partners? Something else? Although the CDO role often focuses on talent management issues, that may not be the only or appropriate focus for your organization. There is no rule to this, other than that you need to be thoughtful about what you are trying to accomplish before you decide about structure and desired outcomes.

One REDI solution does not fit all. You will likely have some unique considerations because of factors such as your industry and the geographic location of headquarters and business units. Take time to think these through. For example, my client in San Francisco focuses more on REDI issues relevant to the needs of Asian Americans and Pacific Islanders and the LGBTQ+ community than on other demographics. My client in Finland operates in a racially homogeneous society but serves clients all over the world, so their REDI focus is broader; they need to understand the rest of the world as much as they need to understand their own society! And the CDO for my client in the advertising business focuses on consumer perceptions above all else. *Now* is the time for *you* to set some intentions that will build an organizational culture in which all employees feel safe and all get about the business of doing their best.

Action #5: Strategically place the CDO (or other REDI leader) in the organization structure

To whom will the CDO report? To you? To the head of HR, or someone else? These might seem like "duh" questions, but the way you answer them will affect who you should select for the job and that person's influence. The structure (form) should follow the purpose (function). You can only define and place the CDO role when you know your REDI BHAG.

Shellye Archambeau advocates a nuanced approach. She said, "Every company is different. It's important that a business focus on its strategy. If a Chief Diversity Officer helps bring more focus to that element of the strategy, then by all means, hire a Chief Diversity Officer. If you don't need that role to drive additional influence, because it's already so fully embedded into the organization, and all your leaders are already thinking like CDOs, that's great, too."

I believe the highest and best use of a CDO is as a "coordinating mechanism"—someone who can aggregate the viewpoints of many decision makers to address collective choice problems. Anything less may not help you make meaningful change. You can learn more about coordinating mechanisms from the work of Dr. Jay Galbraith (see Further Reading).

Action #6: Define the characteristics and success criteria for the CDO role

You need to know what personality traits and skillsets will create success in the CDO role. Mita Mallick provides some helpful guidance (see Further Reading). In my estimation, the most important characteristics for success in this job (because I frame the role as a coordinating mechanism) are a **visionary mindset** (you need a strategist, not a technician), the **listening skills** of a great radio host, the **influence and flesh-pressing skills** of a great politician, and the **"tell-it-like-it-is" confidence** of an activist. You might not need a "spokesperson for the race," a technician, a law expert, or an HR expert (although people with those backgrounds can do this job well if they also have the characteristics I mentioned above).

Set yourself up to get meaningful REDI outcomes by starting with a well-thought-out REDI Vision.

REDI Vision Worksheet

Use this worksheet to organize your thoughts as you prepare to create your REDI Vision. Write your notes in the blank spaces.

REDI Vision action	Current state: What's working well?
1. **Assess:** What would employees say it feels like to work in your company? What would employees of color say? Why?	
2. **Define REDI BHAG:** What is your REDI North Star? What are employees and other stakeholders thinking/saying about the organization's REDI stance?	
3. **Make REDI core to the business:** Which parts of your business need a REDI lens? HR and talent only? Product design? Marketing? Supply chain? Other?	
4. **Define REDI focus:** Respect? Equity? Diversity? Inclusion? All?	
5. **CDO position in the organization structure:** To whom will/does the CDO report?	
6. **Define CDO role (high level):** What will be/is the key focus and what will be/are the required skillsets?	
You: What role are you playing or should you play?	

Current state: What needs attention?	Desired future state: What will you have six or twelve months from now?

EXECUTIVE SUMMARY

- C-suite reactions to REDI strategy will vary, just as representation patterns in their parts of the business may vary.

- CEOs must help the C-suite understand the REDI "why" and lead other decision makers and managers to the necessary mindset.

- Involve the entire C-suite in defining the REDI Vision and hold them accountable for outcomes that support your REDI Vision.

- Define the REDI Vision to lead the rest of the organization.

- Hire the CDO *after* you define the REDI Vision.

REDI QUESTIONS

What is your relationship like with your executive team? Is it collaborative or combative? Do your executives sincerely support REDI work or are they just paying it lip service? What actions or behaviors led you to that conclusion? What would need to change to have an executive team that fully supports REDI work?

8

A CDO with Resources and Political Clout

· · · · · · · · · · · · · · · · · · ·

Once you have a diversity and inclusion vision, you won't be successful if your team is not excited about it. You need a blend that includes "idea people" and people who can execute.

ANDREA HOFFMAN, interview with the author

WAS PRESENTING the results of a research study about leadership coaching effectiveness to a C-suite team at their global company headquarters in Michigan. About five members of the corporate HR department were also in the room, including Jimmy. He listened carefully to what I was saying, and then turned to one of his colleagues and said, "That's really interesting. Do you think this would work for the managers in quality control?" His colleague responded that this was a great idea, and after some collaborative back and forth, we continued the meeting. I was thrilled that Jimmy was so engaged in the conversation. He was the Assistant VP of Talent then, reporting to the company's Chief Human Resources Officer. Too often I had seen people in roles like his miss the opportunity to flex their influence in front of the C-suite. I could tell that Jimmy was going places. Over time we forged a professional relationship, and I became his executive coach. A few years later Jimmy took a CDO position at a global pharmaceuticals company. I was thrilled, yet concerned. To this point his career was progressing in the deliberate fashion he envisioned. I worried that a CDO role could derail Jimmy's CHRO ambitions; many CDOs had told me stories of hard work, frustration, confusion, and disappointment. I did not want that for Jimmy.

When I received an email from Jimmy about six months into his CDO tenure, I couldn't wait to get the scoop.

"Gena, girl, it's crazy over here. I can't figure out if my boss is a genius or a moron. For sure she is 100 percent fake!" Jimmy was the first CDO at the company, reporting to the CHRO. Apparently, she had hired Jimmy because the CEO had insisted she do so, but once Jimmy arrived, she avoided him and refused to provide strategic direction. She even ordered Jimmy not to speak to her C-suite peers unless he "cleared it" with her first. Jimmy was in a no-win situation; he knew that failure was inevitable. After a month or two of this nonsense, Jimmy took matters into his own hands.

On one hand, Jimmy did not want to create a REDI strategy without a sense of how it fit into the larger business strategy. On the other hand, doing nothing was not an option. So, he created a document discussing high-level REDI strategy (based on the input he had collected from conversations with employees at all levels of the organization) and shared it with the CHRO. She blew up. "How dare you create a plan without consulting with me first!" Then she said, "I will review this, but since I did not get approval for the funds I thought we would have, you'll have to figure out which of these things are real priorities and which can wait until next year. This is a well-established company with standard ways of doing things. Your ideas are overly ambitious and don't allow time for the executives to carefully consider all the options. You need to slow down!"

Each night as Jimmy lay awake in bed, he wondered why he had ever taken that job and if he should jump ship before things got worse and his reputation was tarnished inside and outside the company. By the time Jimmy called me, he didn't just want to vent, he wanted me to coach him through this situation, and perhaps onto his next job. I had done this a couple of times with other CDOs, and in Jimmy's case, it quickly became obvious that he was in a no-win situation. Two months later, he left that job and has vowed to never take another CDO position. Good call, in this case. His organization had not set him up for success. His boss, the CHRO, was so afraid to rock the boat at her organization that she was frozen in place, and that meant Jimmy would be frozen too.

A Job Fraught with Landmines

A CDO cannot be successful if those upon whom they depend for political, strategic, and financial support do not yet have a REDI Vision!

Jimmy's story is not uncommon. Many people hired into top REDI roles (regardless of the title) step into situations that feel like covert operations in which the only things executives want is plausible deniability. On one hand, CDOs are asked to lead significant change; on the other, they may not get the ground cover necessary to optimize their impact. The position is often derailed by internal politics and systemic resistance. Is it any wonder that although CDO hiring *has* increased dramatically, turnover among CDOs has *also* increased? Like Jimmy, many departing CDOs say they never enjoyed the influence and authority necessary to make REDI changes.

Do all you can to set your CDO up for success before they even arrive, rather than depending on ad hoc interventions post-hire.

When a CDO's Work on Your REDI Vision Gets Derailed

In researching this book, I spoke with several REDI practitioners and summarized their lessons of experience from their first six months in a CDO or other top-level REDI role. This list does not cover all the ways a CDO could be derailed, but it is food for thought to help you understand how best to set up your CDO role before you even begin to interview candidates.

1   **Flawed reporting structure.** The REDI Vision the C-suite has defined for the business should determine where the CDO role should sit in the organizational structure and to whom the CDO should report. If you want your CDO to play the role of a coordinating mechanism whose influence is felt not just on traditional human resources activities but also on product, marketing, supply chain, and other parts of the business, it makes sense for the CDO to report to the CEO. This direct-to-CEO model also works well if this is the first time REDI will be an enterprise strategic priority, or if you expect the CDO to encounter systemic resistance from other senior leaders. When the CDO reports directly to the CEO, it signals to the entire organization that you mean business.

The REDI lead role is often set up to report to the CHRO, and this structure works when the CHRO is a confident political powerhouse, when REDI issues have already been on the C-suite agenda for many years, or when the organization already has the outlines of a REDI strategy. This structure also works if you only want the CDO to make human resources decisions such as hiring, talent mobility, performance management design, compensation, and so on. One big challenge with the CDO-reporting-to-CHRO model, as Jimmy experienced, is that it fails if the CHRO is threatened by the attention the CDO will inevitably get from the rest of the C-suite.

2 **Unclear mission.** If the CDO's mission is unclear and there is no agreement on how success will be measured, outcomes will at best be mixed.

3 **Lack of executive buy-in.** Your CDO will run into trouble if members of the executive team are only giving lip service to their REDI efforts and do not believe a CDO is needed. The CHRO, Chief Marketing Officer (CMO), head of supply chain, or other top-level leaders whose work should be affected by the REDI strategy should all be required to work in partnership with the CDO from the get-go.

4 **Lack of resources.** If the CDO position is under-resourced financially, politically, or both, you will be setting them up for struggle.

5 **Lack of inclusion.** If your CDO is subjected to the same exclusionary behavior they are asked to fix for the enterprise, they may be robbed of energy to do the work. As Marguerite Ward writes, CDOs often face emotional labor (the need to regulate feelings, reactions, and body language), disrespect, tiredness, and burnout.

The CDO position can be a thankless, soul-crushing job. Ironically, the person the organization hires to lead REDI often bears the emotional brunt of any pushback and is also held accountable for delays, missteps, and over-reach. However, you can circumvent these derailing behaviors and set your CDO up for success!

The CDO's Purpose

Are you hiring your organization's first CDO? If you are, you may be thinking that the job is mostly about providing REDI education and training to the organization. While "training" will surely be a part of your eventual REDI strategy, training is not itself a REDI strategy. Your CDO should ideally be focused on higher-order, strategic impacts rather than on the tactical tools that will be used to deliver that value.

In July 2020, Josh Bersin published research documenting that employees mainly want a CDO to "encourage and engage in dialogue about the systemic racism that holds back minorities and women." This priority was followed by "getting buy-in from change champions, especially White men," and "fixing structural gaps through compensation, hiring, succession, and managerial capability" and "being less scared to discuss race issues." Employees have lofty, strategic expectations for a CDO and are not focused on training. A further complication is that efforts to address these employee expectations are likely to meet resistance because conversations about race and social justice are still not typical in the workplace, and many may actively avoid these topics.

The bottom line is that the CDO's primary job should be to create an environment that supports difficult conversations

The CDO needs the
authority to influence outcomes
in various functions across
the enterprise, not just talent
management outcomes.

that enhance the day-to-day experience of all employees. To do this, the CDO needs the authority to influence outcomes in various functions across the enterprise, not just talent management outcomes. It is critical that you ensure your C-suite has a shared understanding of the REDI Vision and the CDO has a North Star.

Actions to Support the CDO

By now you recognize the need to establish your organization's REDI Vision before the CDO starts their job. Before hiring, you can do the following:

- Complete the REDI Vision work from the previous chapter. (You've probably already done this, but I remind you here because it is the most important action you can take.)

- Ensure that the C-suite is in sync regarding messaging within their areas of responsibility. Speak directly with the heads of HR, marketing, supply chain, and other functional and business units you expect will regularly interact with the CDO. Provide space so their opinions and concerns can be heard. Meet with each, individually, to discuss your expectations for how they will partner with the CDO. Make it clear that the CDO job is not an island and does not "belong" to human resources, even if that is the reporting structure. You want each member of the C-suite to feel they are part of this key decision and that they are expected to partner with the CDO.

- Devise a communication plan regarding the CDO's hire. Focus these communications on providing transparency to employees about the role. Align the communications plan with your REDI Vision. Communicate the "why" to employees before the CDO's first day.

• Define a REDI budget that can accomplish your REDI Vision. Don't make the CDO beg for the resources they need to do the job.

In the first ninety days, support the CDO for success by taking the following actions:

• On day one, announce the CDO's arrival to the organization via your standard communication channels.

• About a week post-hire, introduce the CDO to the company in an all-hands call or other employee event during which you will further explain the REDI Vision at a high level. Do not introduce the CDO as a "savior" or "fixer," but rather as part of your leadership team and someone whose work is meant to improve the overall experience for all employees (and possibly for customers, suppliers, and the community, depending on the scope you define for the job).

• Give the CDO the opportunity to quickly assess the situation and define their priorities, relative to your REDI Vision.

• Invite the CDO to share their initial strategic thoughts with you and the rest of the senior leaders. Then give them space to do their job, being responsive to their requests for resources.

EXECUTIVE SUMMARY

- Complete your REDI Vision before hiring a CDO.

- Define a fit-for-purpose CDO role and let that determine where the position will sit in the organizational structure.

- Set up the CDO role as a strategic partner to all other parts of the business—a coordinating mechanism, not a siloed functionary. Encourage partnership from the start.

- Before and after the CDO begins, lay the groundwork for the ongoing success of the role.

REDI QUESTIONS

What is the best strategic purpose for a CDO in your organization: is it to increase workforce diversity and enhance workforce inclusion, or do you envisage a broader mission for the CDO? What unintended consequences of having a CDO might you anticipate? How will the other members of the C-suite be expected to align their work to the CDO's mission? How will the CDO role relate to your broader ESG work?

9

Meeting in the Middle

. . . .

*If a first-line manager wants to be a second-line manager, but
they cannot demonstrate that they can hire, retain, promote,
or develop a diverse team, they should not get promoted. Train
them and give them some time to get it done, but definitely
do not reward behavior that is opposite of your strategic goals.*

SHELLYE ARCHAMBEAU, interview with the author

'VE SEEN a lot of poor leadership in my years working
directly with global organizations. What do I mean by
"poor" leadership? The world of work has been disrupted
but, whether hybrid, remote, or face-to-face, the fun-
damentals of effective human leadership have not changed
much, from a psychology perspective. I/O psychologist
Dr. Gary Yukl conveniently summarizes most of "what we
know" about leadership in his four-category taxonomy of
leadership behavior. Effective leaders are **task-oriented**
(ensure that people, equipment, and other resources are used
efficiently to accomplish the organization's goals), **relations-
oriented** (enhance team member skills, leader-member relationships, connection, and commitment to the work unit
or organization), **change-oriented** (increase innovation,

learning, and adaptation to changes), and **external-oriented** (provide information about the outside, get resources and assistance, and advocate for the team). So, a "poor" leader, in my opinion, is one who exhibits only a subset of the behaviors in Yukl's model—or who exhibits these behaviors to support only a subset of the people they lead.

These elements of effective leadership matter whether you are leading a team at a start-up or a centuries-old company. The relations-oriented behaviors such as supporting, developing, recognizing, and empowering employees make the biggest difference when it comes to day-to-day employee experience. Unfortunately, according to Gallup's data, only about 20 percent of current managers seem naturally matched to the interpersonal demands of managerial roles. Many employees know they have poor managers, which is why so many are disengaged at work. About 40 percent of employees, regardless of race, say they do not have a sponsor to help them succeed at work. For Black and Hispanic/Latino women, the number increases to 45 percent.

Managers get their lowest effectiveness ratings from employees of color. Why? Research shows a pattern of own-race bias, in which employees have better outcomes when they are the same race as their manager. This pattern is strongest when the relationship is between White managers and White employees. McKinsey's *Race in the Workplace* report confirmed that Black employees do not have the same experiences in the workplace as their White counterparts. Black employees perceive less fairness in the allocation of rewards and fewer chances to succeed. Almost 50 percent of Black respondents said they do not receive support at work to advance in their careers, compared with 39 percent of White employees. Dr. Meisha-ann Martin, senior director of People

Analytics and Research at Workhuman, has observed recognition inclusion gaps for Black and Hispanic men relative to other employees. "These men receive and give less recognition," Meisha-ann said. Workhuman's research shows that individuals who give and receive social recognition are more engaged and less likely to leave the company. Since Black and Hispanic males are at the bottom of the recognition pile, they are likely to have lower feelings of inclusion and higher turnover.

These data make it clear that many managers are not effective at the parts of their job that fall into Yukl's relations-oriented dimension. And that managers can be spectacularly weak at relations-oriented leadership of diverse teams.

It is worth pointing out that since 73 percent of US managers are disproportionally White, many managers lead people who do not look like them. And that managers, regardless of their race, may need more training than you realize to be effective at leading their people, especially those who do not look like them.

100% Leadership

I have experienced, researched, and studied these issues for a long time, and I am convinced that no REDI effort can succeed unless it is built upon a foundation of strong leadership development. CEOs should define what effective leadership looks like in their companies, regarding REDI and all other aspects of leadership. Managers are only effective if they consistently define a positive workplace experience for *everyone* they lead. People of color do not need "special" leadership or more leadership. They need their leaders to provide them

People of color do not
need "special" leadership or
more leadership. They need their
leaders to provide them with
the same support they mete out
to other colleagues but
often withhold from them.

with the same support they mctc out to other colleagues but often withhold from them.

One reason so many employees are dissatisfied with their jobs is that their managers do not pay enough attention to the daily human experience on the teams they lead. REDI requires a new manager mindset about interactions with all employees, especially employees of color. Effective leadership is about attending to the needs of *all* employees, *including* people of color. Inclusive leadership should not be treated like an "add-on"; it is component of effective leadership.

Manager as designated hitter

Baseball's designated hitter (DH) role is a useful analogy for effective REDI leadership. A DH has only one job: to bat in place of the pitcher. There is no hemming and hawing about who is accountable or whether the job is being done well. And the DH does not expect anyone else to do the job.

Few managerial jobs are as clearly defined as that of base-ball's DH, but managerial roles should be that clear. Managers will be more effective if they behave like DHs: remembering that they are the *only* person in the *entire* organization who is primarily responsible for effectively managing each person on their team.

Employees pay close attention to their managers. They know if the manager prefers to wear black shoes or brown shoes and whether they prefer Android or iOS devices. Managers have a metaphorical bullseye in the middle of their foreheads because they are the one person in the entire organization who is designated to be each employee's advocate. If the leader does not do this job like a DH, who else will?

When the manager does not behave like a DH, a leadership void emerges. As is revealed in the McKinsey data, this leadership void is exacerbated for people of color, particularly Black employees. A DH in a REDI context means that a manager uses 100% Leadership—enhancing the experience of each individual employee on the team they lead, regardless of their ethnicity, race, or any other way that humans vary.

The Great ReEsteemation!

According to the November 2018 US Bureau of Labor Statistics' American Time Use Survey, Americans with full-time jobs spent almost 30 percent of each weekday (about nine hours each day) working. Since, as previously noted, employees believe only about 20 percent of current managers are effective, we reach the discomforting conclusion that most employees (about 80 percent) are spending long hours under the leadership of ineffective managers. This is a colossal psychological burden.

In May of 2021, about a year and a half into the COVID-19 pandemic, Texas A&M University organizational psychologist Dr. Anthony Klotz coined the term "the Great Resignation" to describe the phenomenon in which employees were quitting their jobs en masse. The big question was, "*Why?*" Early explanations focused on workers' desire for greater flexibility and autonomy. As time went on, these resignations seemed more like a movement than individual protests. What exactly *were* workers running away from? The resignation phenomenon was affecting all kinds of jobs and industries, including restaurants, healthcare, and technology. In my opinion, Karla Miller's piece in the *Washington Post* hit the nail on the head. Employees were running away from being "micromanaged and disrespected." Employees were not running away from "work," writ large; they were running away from their managers. They were running away from mistreatment that has made them feel undervalued as humans. No amount of flexibility will fix that. Employees want their managers to put them at the core of the work experience.

Therefore, rather than "Great Resignation," I call this phenomenon a Great *ReEsteemation*! Employees are not running *away* from work; they are running *toward* the hope of feeling like whole humans as they do their jobs. Employees are looking at themselves in the mirror and saying, "I am not willing to sell my soul and feel bad about myself just to get a paycheck!" This phenomenon started before the COVID-19 pandemic; the pandemic accelerated its pace and impact. During the Great ReEsteemation, Black employees were the only race/ethnic group that cited personal safety above all other concerns, including covering monthly expenses. You could say that for employees of color, feeling whole at work is as important as getting a paycheck, if not more!

Executive coach Dr. Marilyn Gist, author of *The Extraordinary Power of Leader Humility* and professor emerita and former executive director of the Center for Leadership Formation at Seattle University, noted, "People have three primary questions when facing a... leader: Who *are* you? Where are we *going*? Do you *see me*?" This Great ReEsteemation is every manager's chance to show each employee that they are seen within a large context of purpose and connection.

The REDI Journey: A Marathon, Not a Sprint

There is so much REDI work to be done; we are just getting started. Employees of color have long yearned for many of the changes in corporate America that were spurred, directly and indirectly, by Mr. Floyd's killing.

One day, we will no longer need the term "diversity and inclusion," used within the context of fixing race-based workplace disparities. One day we may not need CDOs! But we are not anywhere near that point. Rather, we are just getting started. There will be many missteps as we all try to get there, together. Along the way, 100% Leadership—in which managers are focused on and accountable for supporting each employee on their team—is vital.

Individual managers will make or break all your REDI efforts. You will need to help each become more effective in leading diverse teams. Here are a few tips to set the stage with managers before you launch your formal REDI strategy:

- Make it clear to all your managers that the REDI work is a priority for you and for them.

- Set the (new) expectation with each manager that 100% Leadership will be required—they must be designated hitters for each member of their team. You will need to support managers via development activities so this way of thinking and acting becomes habitual. Remember, most employees currently perceive most managers as ineffective. And today many managers are getting away with leading only a portion of their teams. You must change that.

- Communicate your high-level REDI Vision to your organization's managers before your CDO starts (or before your REDI strategy is finalized). Give managers a chance to ask questions and to offer input, so they can understand your reasons for this focus (especially if this work is completely new for the organization). Empower them to answer employees' questions to help establish the essential connection between your REDI strategy and their 100% Leadership expectation.

Rather than "Great Resignation,"
I call this phenomenon a
Great *ReEsteemation*! Employees
are not running *away* from
work; they are running *toward* the
hope of feeling like whole
humans as they do their jobs.

- Let managers know that although the CDO will lead the REDI Vision, the CEO and the entire C-suite have skin in the game and will be active partners with the CDO. And make it clear that they (managers) are part of the long-term solution.

- Above all, give managers the chance to keep up with your REDI thinking. Begin the process of "normalizing" REDI and an inclusive culture by talking about it in your standard communications within and outside the business.

Drive Change Employees Can See and Feel

You need your REDI program to make sense to your whole organization. Your primary stakeholder for this work is your *entire employee population*! Although investors and community leaders have a vested interest in this work, it is employees' opinions that will determine if your REDI strategy is successful. Employees will be watching your every move, and they expect you to present a REDI strategy that drives outcomes they can see and feel. You will have only two possible paths to accomplish this: you can influence employees through your direct communications to them and you can influence them through your managers.

No matter how effective your direct communications to employees, you are not in touch with every employee every day. However, your managers do (or at least *should*) have an intimate understanding of employees' day-to-day experiences. You (and your CDO) need to work with managers to deliver your REDI message.

What could possibly go wrong? If the people they lead already question their effectiveness, some of your managers may not be very effective communicators of the REDI strategy. Put another way, inclusive cultures cannot be built if managers are ineffective, because ineffective managers do not practice 100% Leadership. Your organization must have a learning-oriented culture that emphasizes flexibility, open-mindedness, and exploration; it is the only way employees will share their REDI experiences and ideas or believe managers support their career ambitions. Today, only about 30 percent of employees believe their leaders are effective at role-modeling or shaping culture, so there is a lot of work to be done to develop managers so they can effectively support REDI strategy (or any other business strategy, for that matter!).

Your REDI success will depend upon a bedrock of continuous learning for your managers. Your learning plans may already incorporate unconscious bias and anti-racism training, and that is certainly useful for enhancing manager and employee awareness about these issues. However, the additional training your managers need should focus on their becoming more effective as designated hitters for everyone they lead. The most powerful thing you can do is set the expectations for how you want your managers to behave, train them how to behave this way, and then hold them accountable to these behaviors. Make your REDI leadership expectations transparent and required. And teach leaders and managers how to be change agents, too. Employees of all types will see the difference.

Advancing REDI

Once you know what you believe, have a strategic REDI Vision, and know how to start removing the barriers to REDI work through partnership with your executive team, board, and managers, you are more likely to be successful in diversifying the talent in your organization and building an inclusive work culture. And there are many other benefits to this proactive approach:

- Your actions will be perceived as genuine because you will have skin in the game and will be an active part of the solution.

- You are more likely to attract and retain diverse talent.

- Your board of directors and executive team will be more prepared to deal with REDI challenges because they will have been involved in creating the REDI Vision.

- Your executive team and leaders will be more aligned with you and will support this work. Even if their personal experiences and beliefs are not fully aligned, it will be clear to them that you will not tolerate behavior that threatens your REDI intentions. They will emulate what you model.

- This work will enhance your overall leadership effectiveness.

You, rather than your external stakeholders, will control the progress timeline. You will be on your way to making corporate America better, one employee at a time!

Now, it is time to talk about the Action portion of the Inclusion MBA model. I'll do that in the next few chapters.

EXECUTIVE SUMMARY

- Managers can make or break your REDI strategy.

- Use your REDI Vision to effectively frame the "why" for your managers.

- Establish managerial behavior expectations—100% Leadership— as part of your REDI Vision. All employees will benefit from this increased emphasis on humanizing the employee experience.

REDI QUESTIONS

How would you describe the current leadership culture in your organization? Are managers in partnership with those they lead, or do they behave more like "bosses"? Do your managers understand that you require them to be inclusive leaders? Do they know the behaviors they must exhibit to be considered effective in an inclusive leadership environment? Are they held accountable for living up to those expectations?

PART FOUR

ACTION

IT WON'T BE EASY,
BUT IT CAN BE DONE

. . . .

Inclusion Reframe #3: Action

*My organization will only be inclusive
if I drive the change to make it so!*

10

HR and the Science
of Inclusive Leadership

....

*People want microwave solutions to problems
that have been slow-cooked.*
DR. DEREK R. AVERY, interview with the author

MAZON SCRAPPED its artificial intelligence–based recruiting tool in 2018 because it "did not like women,"
as Reuters reported. The tool was not rating candidates in a gender-neutral way because the data used
to build the algorithms was from job applications submitted
to the company in the preceding ten years, most of which
had come from White males. The tool, unwittingly, became
a self-perpetuating maleness machine.

Early in my career, I designed selection systems that
included elements like interview guides, biodata (biographic
facts about the candidate and their opinions and values), cognitive ability tests, and behavioral simulations. I designed
these selection protocols with great rigor, using the results
of formal job analysis to determine which knowledge, skills,
abilities, and other characteristics (psychologists like me call

these KSAOs) differentiated the high performers from those who were less effective in the job for which the selection system would be used. When we measured these differentiators in the selection process, we could predict which candidates were likely to be more effective in the job. Selection systems that do this well are called "valid" predictors because you can see a statistical relationship (usually a correlation) between performance on the selection system and the performance data of the people who are hired. We would evaluate the usefulness of these tests in one of two ways. Either we would give the test to a group of job incumbents of all performance levels to see if the test differentiated between the actual low and high performers, or we would administer the selection protocol to all candidates but continue to select them based on separate tools that were already being used (for example, traditional interview judgments). We would put the test scores away and wait until the hires performed in the job for a while (typically, about a year). Then we analyzed the data to see if the unused test scores could have predicted the higher performers from the others. We expected to see, and usually found, that those who scored higher on the tests also scored higher on job performance measures.

I have always advised HR and other corporate leaders that decisions such as who gets a job (or not), who is promoted (or not), and who is selected for the leadership training program (or not) should only be made based on a thorough understanding of the job and on valid decision-making criteria. By "criteria" I mean the "standard" against which success is judged. Supervisory ratings of job performance are the most commonly used performance criteria. (Note: Since supervisory performance ratings can be problematic, psychologists doing selection validation work create special

performance ratings and do not use the company's performance rating tools.)

Many clients realize that federal legal guidelines cover the
use of tests for point-of-hire decisions but do not realize that
these laws also apply to other selection decisions (such as
who gets selected for a training program or who gets promoted). A "test or selection procedure" is not just a hiring
test. It might be a post-training evaluation, a performance
appraisal procedure, or any other tool or procedure used for
a variety of talent decisions.

Therefore, my standard talent selection guidance is
straightforward and consistent:

- Define the criteria you will use to make talent decisions
  before, not after, you see the candidates.

- Make talent decisions based on data, preferably on judgments from more than one person, and not solely on the
  whims of individual managers.

- Use a consistent approach. Even if it is not formally validated by an I/O psychologist, a consistent approach
  will enable you to understand why you did what you
  did, to explain what you did to anyone who challenges
  you (hopefully not in court), and, best of all, to explain
  to the candidate (for example, a candidate for promotion)
  why they did or did not get the opportunity and what they
  can do to prepare themselves the next time the opportunity arises.

When my clients used these practices, they would get
higher on-the-job performance, reduce the risk of discrimination challenges, and better understand the characteristics of
those who were being selected for these opportunities versus

those who were not. And even losing candidates would feel the decision processes were fair.

And yet, this was a hard sell for some of my clients who simply would not do it (those are no longer my clients). Some would say it was too expensive to implement robust selection protocols. Others wanted the easiest and quickest ways to make talent decisions, so they scorned measuring the statistical relationship between outcomes of their selection decisions and the on-the-job performance of those who were hired, promoted, or added to the fast track.

My frustration with the reality I just described is one reason I eventually got out of selection assessment work. Another reason was that, as technology evolved, many of the new tools don't pass muster from an I/O psychology perspective. Dr. Walter "Wally" Borman, a performance measurement expert, was my major professor, and I imagine him cringing when he reads about how some of the new tools are designed. Dr. Paul E. Spector, another of my profs (and a prolific I/O psychologist and business and management scientist ranked among the top 2 percent of scientists in his field), also influences my thinking about this work. These tools are marketed with great gusto by start-up geniuses; we just need to make sure that fairness, access, and opportunity are built in.

The widespread adoption of artificial intelligence (AI) in HR tech is inevitable. Understandably, HR users like the scale, speed, and decision support AI offers. However, users should insist that developers are transparent about how the algorithms function and whether they have an adverse impact on certain candidates as a function of race, gender, or other human variation. That opacity is a concern when AI is used for employee selection. While these tools make recruiters' lives easier by quickly processing large volumes of candidate information, many such tools have been validated on candidate pools that are not representative of the US population. When these tools are used in a country in which race-based subordination is already such a challenge, users must be vigilant to ensure the tools do not reinforce and replicate those subordinations. The guidance from the Society for Industrial and Organizational Psychology (SIOP) is a great resource for evaluating AI-based HR tools.

I am not against AI, but I am *for* greater AI transparency. That is why I was delighted when, in November 2021, the City of New York passed legislation regulating the use of AI in hiring processes. Hopefully, this legislation will drive the national conversation to ensure that AI always comes with disclosures about what is inside the "black box." In January 2022, the Business Roundtable launched a "Roadmap for Responsible Artificial Intelligence (AI)" that will also help drive equitable outcomes from the use of AI-powered HR tech.

I get a little grumpy when clients discuss REDI as if the people, the issues, and the science is something new. It is even more disconcerting to encounter HR professionals—often the first point of contact with candidates of color, and the arbiters of our day-to-day workplace experiences—whose actions are not guided by the relevant psychological science. I don't meet a lot of these science ignorers, but I meet more than I should.

Sometimes executives are not focused on the science, either. Over the years, I offered guidance to executives that was grounded in data and psychological science. Sometimes the data came from research in peer-reviewed journals, sometimes from national academic conferences, and sometimes from applied research conducted in a specific client's workforce (for example, employee opinion surveys and analysis of

I am not against AI,
but I am *for* greater
AI transparency.

archival operations data). I consistently noticed that although business leaders would insist that I base my insights on data, they often made decisions that ignored the implications of the evidence I provided. Although some did this intentionally, most did not even realize this was happening. These leaders would say they were data-driven but, at best, they were "data-ish leaders."

Data Collection

Clarify your REDI questions

It will be hard to take the correct REDI action if you don't know what employees think about their day-to-day work experience. You can address that challenge with robust employee data collection using your own internal employee opinion measurement teams or the guidance of I/O psychologists or others trained in data collection and analysis. When your team collects employee opinion data, tell them, "I depend on you to tell it to me like it is. Don't hold anything back!" The last thing you want is sifted employee opinion data.

I also recommend two other considerations before the data collection begins:

1 What are the key REDI questions swirling in your mind for which you want answers? For example, "Are employees in one group having a different experience than others and, if so, what causes that difference?"

2 Which groups in the organization are of interest when you think about these questions? Women? People of color? Sales team? And so on. For example, if yours is a

global organization, you will need to know if employee . experience varies by location. It would also be misleading to look at the data solely from the perspective of the overall global population or "headquarters."

Make sure you get insights with the level of detail that matches the questions that are swirling in your head. You need that specificity to effectively drive REDI change.

Beware "data-ish" leadership

Many of my clients conduct annual employee opinion surveys to get a baseline measure of employee experience. If an annual survey is all you can do, that is better than nothing. However, in this fast-paced, disrupted digital environment, you should aim to measure employee sentiment more often; a year is too long.

Annual surveys were de rigueur pre-COVID and pre-ReEsteemation, and results were mostly consistent year over year. My clients would keep doing new surveys and getting mostly the same results. When I asked, "What actions did you take since getting the previous year's survey feedback?" the answers would reveal that very little had been done. Sometimes clients had even done the opposite of what I recommended! Often, all the effort to ask employees their opinions was not being matched by a concomitant level of action.

Why would executives expect to get better employee opinion feedback when they were not taking actions based on the data-based insights and recommendations from these surveys? Employee research experts have pondered this question for a long time and consistently conclude that "getting the right results into the right hands and then getting leaders to use these insights will remain our focus for the foreseeable future." Make sure you are not one of those leaders who ask for data-based action recommendations but fail to act on them! Employees will notice right away, and they will be less trusting of your REDI strategy.

You should also make sure the insights and recommendations you receive are thorough and complete. Some HR leaders screen culture and employee opinion data and decide what should be kept, toned down, or deleted before it is delivered to the C-suite. They do this ostensibly to protect your time and sometimes to avoid being the bearers of "bad news." But then you get watered-down insights and take ineffectual actions that contradict the data. You need the whole story: good, bad, and ugly! Otherwise, you will be making *data-ish* decisions that will not have the impact employees are waiting to see and feel.

Be skeptical of historical trends and benchmark comparisons

FantasyCo, Inc. is an amalgam of global clients I advised during the last ten years. FantasyCo ran an annual employee survey around the same time each year, usually asking the same questions from year to year. Each year I advised them to ask questions that mattered in that moment, even if that meant deleting or changing some of the core questions. They would resist, saying, "We need history, so we don't want to change the survey questions! Plus, we want to compare our employees' answers against employee responses from other companies like ours (benchmarks), so we must ask the same questions those companies asked." FantasyCo often seemed more interested in trends and benchmark comparisons than in what their employees were experiencing.

The problem is that, while historical trend comparisons and "benchmark" comparisons can be helpful, they can also be very misleading when used without contextual framing.

When "conditions on the ground" change dramatically from week to week, month to month, and year to year, as they have since the start of 2020, historical trend data and benchmark comparisons must be recalibrated. The workplace has been so disrupted by COVID-19 that we cannot just compare pre-pandemic employee opinion scores to post-pandemic data and think we have an accurate measure of how or if sentiment has changed. The same is true about REDI data. Since stakeholders' expectations have changed, we cannot simply compare pre–May 2020 employee opinion scores to post–May 2020 data and think we have an accurate measure of how or if sentiment has changed. We need a new baseline. For REDI work in this environment, I recommend that you focus less on comparisons to the past and more on understanding the "now."

Similarly, comparing employee opinion scores from one organization to another is an opportunity for gross misinterpretation. Even if employees answered the same questions, no two companies' business strategies, cultures, or management practices are the same. Benchmark comparisons, though interesting, are of questionable value, particularly in a disrupted work world.

If you use surveys as part of your REDI assessment, focus more on the current employee experience (in other words, the current scores) in your own organization than on comparisons to other company's scores.

Race and ethnicity:
Often under-measured and misunderstood

Although there is a generally shared understanding in the US of how race and ethnicity might be defined (typically according to the US Census race and ethnicity classifications), your organization may not have been consistently collecting or analyzing data by race, ethnicity, or other ways in which your workforce might vary. Or the data might have been collected but not shared with you.

Internal survey program managers often share these data and their implications with heads of REDI programs, employee resource groups, and other targeted groups—but not executive leadership. This is a mistake. You may not want the same level of detail as your CDO, but you need to see some specifics.

The impact of failures to collect or adequately break out race and ethnicity data came to the forefront nationally and globally during the COVID-19 pandemic. As public health researchers Farah Kader and Clyde Lanford Smith point out, "Missing data on race/ethnicity from federal, state, and local agencies impede nuanced understanding of health disparities." The corollary is the same for the workplace. Detailed analysis of workplace data, using race and ethnicity and intersectional breakouts, is essential to effective REDI work.

Employee opinion survey scores tend to vary significantly by race, ethnicity, and gender, and tend to be highest for White employees. Additionally, scores for Hispanic/Latino employees tend to look more like the scores of White employees than those of Black or Asian employees. Black employees' scores tend to be lowest on questions about opportunities for growth and development, manager effectiveness, and trust in senior leadership. Therefore, it is insufficient to just look at aggregated employee survey data. Your REDI Vision pre-work should include examining employee opinion data by the variations that exist in your workforce. Insist on seeing the insights by race, gender, and intersectional groupings.

You may think, for legal reasons, that avoiding race- and ethnicity-based patterns in your workforce data is a good idea. But you need that data to accurately measure the outcomes from your REDI work. Even if your HR department has not been providing you with these data, your company is probably already providing data to the federal government via the EEO-I form. The availability of these high-level data breakouts is evidence that it is possible (though not always easy) to collect or extract the race and ethnicity metrics you will need for REDI work.

Black, Hispanic/Latino, and AAPI: Not a monolith

Although it is acceptable to use the term "people of color" as a shorthand way to differentiate between White employees and those who identify with other races or ethnic groups, that convenient shorthand is not helpful for guiding REDI strategy. "People of color" groups together people who have widely disparate cultures, histories, and current experience. Hispanics/Latinos, Asian Americans and Pacific Islanders, Native Americans, and Black Americans each have unique histories, day-to-day experiences, and variations of culture and experience *within* their identity groups.

The Black population and workforce in the US is diverse, whether examined from the perspective of place of origin, US geography, race, ethnicity, appearance, income, education, or other social and economic measures. Similarly, although convenient, the AAPI label describes a diverse population of about 24 million Americans that spans about fifty ethnic groups. And although we use the classification "Hispanic/ Latino" in the US Census and in employee opinion research, there is really no such thing as "Latinos" in the sense of shared experience.

Board director Tricia Montalvo Timm is writing a book about how authenticity can power personal and work success. In an interview with me, she noted that "people from places as diverse as Mexico, Puerto Rico, Colombia, the Dominican Republic, and Cuba get lumped together. But each place has different cultures, mannerisms, foods, and belief systems." She pointed out, for example, that Black people from the Dominican Republic get challenged in the US when they speak Spanish because underinformed people have a stereotype for "Latino-looking people" and do not associate people of African descent with that identity. Timm says, "All of this is about stereotyping. And all of this needs to be changed."

In many race and ethnic groups, lighter skin is perceived to be more desirable than darker skin. Fordham University law professor Tanya K. Hernández pointed out in a powerful 2021 essay that "when provided the ability to check as many racial boxes as apply... a majority of Latinos... prefer to solely check white." She also explains that some Hispanics/Latinos associate lighter skin with "*adelantando la raza*" (improving the race). According to Hernández, "For (some) Latinos in the United States... anything other than black is preferable," referencing a quote from Marta Cruz-Janzen. In other words, *some* "people of color" have the option to be "White" and may be perceived by those in the reference group as White. Those employees' experiences are more like those of the reference group than those of people with darker skin. Black people can also be biased against darker skin—a phenomenon termed "colorism."

So, the term "people of color" is a description without any real value when it comes to understanding employee experience. For REDI work, it is necessary to understand the historical and social differences both within and across "people of color."

Pay attention to employee comments

I attended a session called "The Science of Bouncing Back from Adversity" at the 2021 annual conference of the American Psychological Association. The panel included six PhD psychologists and one non-psychologist, Glynn Washington, the host, creator, and executive producer of the podcast *Snap Judgment*. He shared a story about the unique psychological challenge of dealing with the COVID-19 pandemic for people who had previously endured other trauma. He was there to remind attendees that psychology is most effective when psychologists are informed by the day-to-day experiences of those it seeks to serve.

A few minutes into Washington's remarks, a PhD psychologist in the audience kept asking: "Where is the science?" This person meant, "Why is Mr. Washington talking? He is not a psychology scholar and he is not reporting 'research.'" This interrupter did not seem to understand that the human experience is the very thing that matters in psychology (and in leadership)! He likely did this because, apart from being rude, he is of a generation of psychologists who has focused disproportionately on quantitative data (responses to scaled "agree/disagree" scales, for example) and less so on qualitative data (information in non-numeric form, usually textual or narrative).

I have seen the same underutilization of employee comments in the corporate environment. Although most employee surveys gather both quantitative and qualitative data, the qualitative data (comments) tend to be underexamined and under-shared. And yet, the employee experience is "hidden in plain sight" in those comments. You should insist on seeing analyses of your employees' survey comments, cut by the demographics of interest—including, of course, race and ethnicity and relevant intersectional identities.

When your team collects
employee opinion data,
tell them, "I depend on you
to tell it to me like it is.
Don't hold anything back!"

You can't talk to every employee individually, but employee survey comments can help you understand what is in each employee's heart and suggest the most meaningful actions.

Don't Let the Race and Ethnicity "Taboo" Derail REDI

Scientists have noted that "the explicit discussion of race and organizational leadership is still considered taboo or irrelevant in many business circles." In March 2021, Pew Research documented that "there are wide differences in how Americans view the need for attention to issues of race." Although 97 percent of Black Americans say they experience "a lot" of discrimination in society today, only 40 percent of White Americans believe Black people have that experience. Additionally, although 75 percent of Black Americans say that heightened attention to this topic is good, only 46 percent of White Americans agree. Momentive's 2021 research revealed that only 48 percent of White executives believed that "DEI [diversity, equity, and inclusion] initiatives are an important factor in our company's ability to drive success," while 51 percent of White executives agreed with the statement, "DEI initiatives are a distraction from our company's real work."

Since conversations about race are "taboo" in broader society, you might be reluctant to talk about these subjects yourself. You need to counter this resistance and model the way for those you lead.

Handling bias deniers
Recently a friend and fellow organizational psychologist posted a message on LinkedIn asking how to advise leaders when employees report in employee surveys that they are

experiencing conscious bias and bigotry in the workplace. The subtext of that question was, "What if the leaders do not believe the employee feedback?"

Some leaders and managers in your organization may deny that bias exists, even when employees report having those experiences. If this happens, you must tell those bias deniers that the company believes (1) that no employee should be the victim of intentional or unconscious bias at work, (2) that employees who say they are having these experiences must be assured that their situation will be investigated, and (3) that leaders and HR will resolve any problems identified from the investigations.

You may also discover that some employees (even managers) have been exhibiting biased behaviors in their treatment of some of their colleagues. You don't need to change their beliefs, but you do need to let them and all other employees know you will not tolerate racism, sexism, ableism, heterosexism, and other discriminatory behavior in your organization. Do not allow anyone who contradicts that expectation (even other executives) to remain in the organization. Employees who experience the behaviors that signal bias, such as stereotyping, hostility, overly critical evaluations, and being consistently overlooked for opportunities, are watching and waiting for you to create the changes that will eliminate those behaviors. If they do not see and feel those changes, your REDI work will not succeed.

Advice from Top REDI Scholars

I asked four REDI experts to share their insights about what really works when it comes to driving meaningful REDI change. These four are in positions where they see a wide range of challenges that leaders face in the REDI domain. They are also actively involved in using psychological science to influence practical actions in the world of work. Each is in touch with both psychological science and the zeitgeist.

Dr. Calvin Lai is assistant professor of Psychological and Brain Sciences at Washington University in St. Louis. His research focuses on learning how implicit biases change, understanding the consequences of implicit biases on behavior, and developing interventions to reduce the impact of those biases on behavior. Dr. Lai is known for his application of psychological science to real-world challenges.

Dr. Derek R. Avery is the C.T. Bauer Chair of Inclusive Leadership at the University of Houston and the Diversity and Inclusion Portfolio Officer of the Society for Industrial and Organizational Psychology. Dr. Avery is a thoughtful and energetic researcher and business advisor with an engaging way of communicating big ideas from psychological science. He is among the group of psychologists who rightly lament that race and ethnicity are under-studied, even within the academy of psychological science.

Dr. Kecia M. Thomas is the Dean of the College of Arts and Sciences, University of Alabama at Birmingham (UAB). On one hand, Dr. Thomas is all business; on the other, she laughs loudest at a good joke. She is one of the "coolest" researchers you will meet. Dr. Thomas's influential role within the UAB system reflects her long-term, scaled efforts to support diversity in STEM workplaces through a combination of leadership, science, and social justice advocacy.

Dr. Tiffany Jana (they/them) is the founder and CEO of TMI Portfolio, a collection of companies working to advance inclusive workplaces. They are the author of four popular books on matters related to diversity and inclusion and purposeful business. Dr. Jana is a high-energy and uber-generous person who laughs easily but is not afraid to speak their truth.

I distilled my highly engaging conversations with these four colleagues into the following pointers about what works, from a leadership perspective, when it comes to REDI.

Make it okay to talk about race in your organization

Dr. Thomas noted, "People of color have been suffering race-based indignities, yet they have come to work and done their jobs anyway. Leaders need to match that commitment. And if you're not willing to do that, you cannot expect to become the trusted and inclusive leader you aspire to be. **We need leaders to be brave.**" Allison Manswell, author of *Listen In: Crucial Conversations on Race in the Workplace*, made a similar point years ago: "Not talking about race actually increases the sense of bias somebody already has ... ignoring race can exacerbate rather than alleviate issues of race in the workplace."

Lead REDI strategically

Dr. Jana recommended, "Move away from performative diversity work, and from any temporary, superficial quick fix. That kind of thinking just causes harm. **Look at this work from a systems perspective, and make it sustainable.** Establish something that is long term and that cannot be defunded."

Dr. Thomas added, "I ask clients **to identify a goal for their organization and try to map out the strategy for how the organization can accomplish it**. And I also have them do the same regarding an individual plan. What can you commit to do based upon the new knowledge you have acquired from your training and education efforts?"

Seek systemic, long-term solutions

Dr. Lai pointed out that the implicit bias training that is readily available is not standardized: some of it is very good, and some of it is less so. There is no problem in using that kind of training to raise employee awareness and build more positive attitudes. However, since the outcome you really desire is prolonged behavioral change, you need to manage your expectations about one-off training. On one hand, you should not expect the same results from a two-hour training session as from more robust, data-based diversity and inclusion initiatives, such as changing the composition of an entire entering class of new hires or defining a new inclusive leadership behavior model. On the other hand, **know that the more significant, potentially more influential initiatives will take longer to show their impact. You need both short- and long-term efforts.** Coqual recently introduced a tool, the "Black Equity Index," that can help you track the effectiveness of your race-based REDI efforts.

Establish fairness and inclusion as bedrock principles

"Somebody's got to be the first to say, 'You know what, we're going to fundamentally do this differently than everyone else has from the ground up,'" Dr. Avery said. "'We are going to **build an organization that is committed to fairness and inclusion as bedrock principles.**'" This can only happen if you are willing to withstand the short-term pain that will come from those who say that business should not deal with social concerns. You must decide where you stand.

Focus on diversity and on building inclusive organizational cultures

It is not enough to go out and hire people in all their variations. You should simultaneously **create an environment** where everybody can contribute to their potential, be developed to their potential, and be rewarded based on their contributions and not on their characteristics. A fair, inclusive environment will attract, engage, and retain the best and brightest in all our variations, according to Dr. Avery.

Challenge underlying default assumptions

Make it a habit to challenge any underlying assumptions about what makes a "good" candidate or employee. Dr. Avery noted that traditional hiring and advancement practices tacitly reward jobs and promotions to people who look like the people doing the hiring and promoting. This means that straight, cisgender White males tend to be "the standard," and everyone else needs to justify their candidacy. Leaders must challenge that assumption every time it shows up. Dr. Avery referenced the work of now-deceased Columbia Business School professor Dr. Katherine W. Phillips, a pioneering researcher in how organizations can optimize the talent of employees from diverse backgrounds.

Treat REDI as an essential business competency

Multicultural competency should be an essential leadership expectation, like financial and marketing acumen. CDOs can help with this. As Dr. Thomas put it, "A good CDO can advise and coach their CEO to develop their multicultural consciousness." Don't hire, promote, reward, or retain people who do not have this competency. Do not put people on boards who cannot relate to people who do not look like them or who have no interest in the concerns of people who do not look like them. If you have people like this on your team now, give them time to get up to speed, and then, if they are not prepared to meet these new expectations, let them go.

Manage your own implicit bias

At the individual level, think before you act: implicit bias is real. However, according to Dr. Lai, "We're more likely to act on implicit biases when we don't give ourselves time to think things through." He recommends the same advice your mother likely gave you: **"Think before you speak or make judgments."** You will become a better decision maker and will make fewer biased decisions based on natural human characteristics. At the system and policy level, initial reactions are likely to be informed by implicit biases, too. So, when you need to make (any) crucial decisions (including those where race is involved), you are likely to make better, less biased decisions when you have time to think them through, rather than relying on first impressions.

Manage bias in talent decisions

According to Dr. Lai, one of the best ways to counter bias in talent decisions is for leaders to **avoid making critical talent decisions when they are distracted by other concerns, are tired, or do not have enough time to adequately consider the decision criteria.** He offers the following additional tips to enhance decision making and counter cognitive biases in talent decision making:

- Avoid *starting* the decision-making process with a free-for-all group meeting. Rather, let participants decide independently, outside a group meeting, to minimize groupthink in making big decisions (for example, hiring the first Black woman to your executive team).

- Ask each stakeholder to each record their judgment anonymously on a piece of paper or digital tool. Aggregate the findings and have someone announce the decision based on the aggregation of the individual judgments. This approach makes it easier for participants to express their opinions independently, without being influenced by others' judgments.

* Discuss and make the final decision as a group. Always make talent decisions on valid criteria that matter, such as performance ratings and potential ratings—never on race.

Make data-based talent decisions at all phases

As Dr. Lai put it, "You might be super-invested in reducing bias in your interviewing process, but the bias might not be there; it might be in mobility and retention. That's why it's vital to get the specific numbers and data, just like you would any other type of metric." The point here is that you should **not assume where the problem lies, nor should you assume that you already know the best solution. Let the data inform both the problem-definition and the creation of solutions.**

Build authentically inclusive leaders for the long run

According to Dr. Avery, you must **build systems of compliance and accountability into critical talent decisions.** For example, managers have power when it comes to hiring, promotion, project assignments, and so on. Train them to make fair decisions, and then hold them accountable for doing so. We know from psychology that it is easier to change behavior than to change attitudes—*and* that behavior can change attitudes. So when you focus on systemic behavior change, you may also change attitudes. This is an imperfect approach because some people will only do these "right" things when you force them to. Some managers will circumvent these requirements if they want to sabotage your efforts, so you can't "set it and forget it." As a result, you must set up sustainable accountability processes.

Embrace differences rather than seeking sameness

The benefits of diversity in the natural world suggest that diversity, not homogeneity, is essential for human survival. Dr. Phillips believed that "homogeneity," not "diversity," is the exception and would ask, "What small change can we make as individuals to capture the benefits of diversity?" **Fight the impulse to seek out commonalities with those you encounter and instead "embrace your differences"** by talking about contrasting life experiences. "The environment you will create will be one where difference is normal," according to Dr. Phillips.

Model the way

Racial bias is contagious. Likewise, egalitarian bias can also be contagious. The more you exhibit egalitarian behavior, the more likely it is that observers (other employees, for example) will copy those behaviors. You need to **model the way.**

Find and dismantle race-based siloes in your organization

According to Dr. Thomas, "There are functional areas in organizations where we are more likely to find people of color and women, and other areas where we find very few people of color or women." Both situations are likely outcomes of biased decision making. **Departments and groups that over-index on talent from women and traditionally subordinated groups tend to have lower pay and fewer mobility options.** And this becomes a self-fulfilling pattern as men and those with social power avoid these groups. **Break up those patterns and systems.** Where women and people of color are underutilized, require the leaders to identify and communicate back the explanations for the underrepresentation.

Then, require them to present plans redressing the problem. Require them to advertise available opportunities to
the entire organization and recruit from outside their familiar network or colleges. This will split up the power cliques.
Train leaders to identify and document the career aspirations
of each person on their teams, and provide coaching so team
members can be developed for new opportunities. Redesign the work in those groups to make those opportunities
attractive to a wider range of applications, and re-evaluate the
criteria for candidacy to make sure people who can do the job
are not being ruled out for invalid reasons.

Support anti-racism mechanisms inside and outside the organization

As discussed throughout this book, our society is highly
segregated by race and ethnicity. Until that changes, the
workplace may be the only place many in your workforce regularly encounter a wide variation of humankind. Additionally,
some employees' day-to-day experiences outside work may
expose them to people and ideas that run counter to your
company's anti-racism, anti-sexism, anti-ableism, and anti-
heterosexism efforts. **You can't change peoples' personal
beliefs, but you can start by using words that clearly state
what you are *for* and what you are *against*** and use those values to determine who should remain or become part of your
great organization.

Multicultural competency should be an essential leadership expectation, like financial and marketing acumen.

What Does Not Work for REDI

Quick fixes

Racism has been present for centuries. It will take time to find the solutions to "fix" discrimination in the workplace. The effective solutions will not be one-size-fits-all, either. As Dr. Avery noted, throwing money at the problem by saying, "'We're going to hire somebody,' or 'we're going to outsource this function,' or 'we're going to invest in this short-term training initiative'" will not work. **You need a long-term strategy against which you can progress consistently and visibly.**

Expecting the CDO to "just handle it"

As Dr. Thomas noted, CDOs and other diversity and inclusion practitioners report that executives try to position them as the REDI "fixer." That will never work. CDOs can be a critical part of the solution, but their key role should be as a strategic partner to other business leaders. Otherwise, as reported in *Business Insider*, **"When corporate executives fail to support their DEI colleagues, not only do DEI leaders have to engage in high emotional labor, but they also experience a loss in motivation."**

All talk, no action

Research from Berkeley business school psychology professor Dr. Drew Jacoby-Senghor and his colleagues found that "the explicit goal of appearing egalitarian might blind people to the possibility that they could be communicating, and perpetuating, prejudicial attitudes." A key lesson in this: "Words carry weight. **You can unwittingly spread prejudice when you give lip service to REDI work but take no real action."** Action is always more valuable more than talk.

Copying what other organizations do

Companies that receive REDI awards surely deserve them for the things they are doing right. However, what one company does might be the opposite of what would work for your company. Although you can adopt some best practices, avoid copying without understanding the context. There is no substitute for a strategy driven by your organization's unique values, products and services, and customers. No matter what approach you take, you should not expect 100 percent success, especially not on the first efforts. That does not happen with any other kind of work, and it won't happen with REDI. However, when you tailor your efforts to your organization's uniqueness, employees are more likely to understand the "why" and to support you. And you will retain employee support even if you sometimes stumble. **Take a custom approach that is purposeful, consistently applied, sustainable, and tied to your REDI strategy.**

Overreliance on AI in talent systems

Dr. Jana shares my earlier caution about using AI for talent systems. They say that if people who code the algorithms all come from one walk of life, the experience they encode into the product may show up as bias against those who have had a different lived experience. **When you buy AI, don't just focus on the function, also focus on who is making it, and on their REDI values.**

Put Me in the Game and Show Me the Money

Career mobility and compensation equity are two specific outcomes you should focus on in your REDI work. Traditionally, processes for compensation decisions have been opaque, while managers have had a lot of discretion in how they allocate these resources.

In my own experience, some HR leaders and hiring managers will offer lower pay rates, pay increases, and performance incentives to people of color than what is offered to their counterparts. A 2021 Coqual study revealed that many employees of color perceive that we wait longer for promotion opportunities than White employees. One contributing factor is that managers' evaluations of our performance may not adequately reflect our contributions. (You can refer to Chapter 4 for a more detailed discussion of the science regarding this issue.) Another contributing factor is the persistent and systemic under-leveling of certain functions and jobs. According to Maria Colacurcio, CEO of pay equity innovator Syndio, an example of this is that "HR tends to be... the most undervalued function, and it also tends to be the one with the most women and people of color in leadership roles." **You will have made meaningful REDI progress when people of color are represented in the higher level and more influential roles that have not traditionally welcomed us, and when the roles that have traditionally welcomed us are not systemically undervalued.**

Be sure to also scrutinize how managers determine and allocate compensation. Women still earn less than men (about 84 cents for each dollar), and intersectional pay gaps persist. College-educated Black and Hispanic men earn about 80 percent of what White college-educated men earn, and Black and Hispanic women earn about 70 percent of that. Maria makes two recommendations to help address these inequities: (1) analyze compensation data using both race/ethnicity and gender and the intersection of the two, and (2) analyze all aspects of compensation. Include incentives and equity/stock option allocations, and not just base pay.

"The successful twenty-first-century company will be measuring workplace (pay) equity and doing so more often," according to Maria.

The REDI actions that make sense for your organization will be unique. However, the experts in this chapter provided directional guidance, pointing you to three key focus areas: **strategic leadership**, **REDI leader support**, and **talent decision process improvement** (including selection, performance measurement, promotions and career mobility, and compensation).

EXECUTIVE SUMMARY

- Effective REDI solutions should be built upon data-based insights that show leaders what matters most. Ad hoc actions may not hurt but may result in disappointing outcomes or unintended negative consequences.

- To get valid REDI data insights, leaders must ensure that insights your advisors provide are disaggregated in a way that will enable you to see the patterns by the demographics that matter in your organization.

- Although REDI solutions need to be customized for each company, the psychological science indicates that there are some best practices any company can implement to positively influence systemic bias in talent systems.

REDI QUESTIONS

What is the basis, in data, for the guidance you are currently receiving about REDI work in your organization? Is your organization using the practices that are known to work and avoiding those that do not? How is your organization defining the success of its REDI work? What accountability mechanisms are in place to ensure that managers' actions are aligned with your REDI expectations? Has any manager in your organization been out of compliance with these expectations? If so, what repercussions did they experience? How will you know which of the REDI actions you are taking are making a difference for your employees?

11

Seeing All Women Clearly

· · · · · · · · · · · · · · · · · · · ·

For too long we have positioned women as a
deviation from standard humanity and this is why they
have been allowed to become invisible. It's time for
a change in perspective. It's time for women to be seen.
CAROLINE CRIADO PEREZ, *Invisible Women*

RIOR TO BECOMING an equity, diversity, and social
impact workplace consultant in Geneva, Switzerland,
Tom Waterhouse spent more than thirty years in
corporate roles. Once, while working for a European
organization in which the top fifty leaders were all White
males, he submitted a perfectly matched female candidate
for a position on his team. HR's response was, "She's French,
she's Catholic, she's a *woman*. Why would you want to hire
her?" Tom hired her anyway, and she spent a highly successful decade at the company, during which she also met and
married her husband and had four children. The company
also had a rule that if you moved to part-time (as some moth-
ers and caregivers needed to do), you would automatically
lose your VP title. Tom pointed out that this rule was biased
against women, but the company could not see it. They kept

saying, "It is just a policy and it applies to everyone, so it can't be discriminatory."

As Tom put it, "Men are often in denial about the extent to which the women around them are subject to sexism, harassment, and discrimination on a daily basis." As you read this you might think, "Those examples are extreme; they would never happen in my organization." And yet, although women's representation has increased across the talent pipeline since 2016, women remain significantly underrepresented in leadership. Women of color are still underrepresented at every level in the corporate structure, and that underrepresentation is worse at higher levels.

A Large Part of the REDI Story

As Caroline Criado Perez made clear in her groundbreaking treatise *Invisible Women*, women are so invisible that our needs and experiences are often underrepresented in data and, therefore, underrepresented in leadership, policy, and even product design decisions. We are in the world (of work), but the world (of work) does not factor us in 50/50 relative to our male counterparts! Gender bias is so entrenched that it can go unnoticed, right in front of our eyes.

Imagine what it must be like, then, for women of color who experience gender discrimination to the second power—with a layer of racial discrimination added to sexism. As discussed in Chapter 10, the terms "people of color," "Asian American and Pacific Islander," "Hispanic/Latino," and "Black/African American" are not perfect, but they are a convenient way to focus on the differentiated experiences of women of color at work. Take the time to notice the variations within these groupings. Remember that each person represented by their grouping is an individual who wants nothing more than to be seen, heard, and valued for their unique humanity.

The Unique Experiences of Women of Color

Deepa Purushothaman, cofounder of nFormation.com and author of *The First, the Few, the Only*, shared some of her research findings regarding women of color, especially those at higher levels in corporate America. Published in partnership with the Billie Jean King Leadership Initiative, this research is detailed in the report *PowHER Redefined*. The main finding was that women of color believe current models of leadership do not work for everyone, and especially do not work for us. These women reported that there is little room for our full voice, our full contribution, and our authenticity at tables of power. Aware that we will never behave like a White-male-centered definition of what good leadership looks like, women of color are seeking to change that model so that leadership can work for everyone. Women of color are looking for space to redefine what effective leadership looks like, according to Deepa.

A pattern of biased reactions at work

Women of color experience some unique discriminatory responses at work. Black women are treated somewhat condescendingly—like a "pet" early in our careers, and like a "threat" as soon as we become more confident or express ambitions. This "pet to threat" syndrome was documented in 2013 in Dr. Kecia Thomas's research. AAPI women deal with the "exotic model minority myth," which causes others to undervalue them as managerial talent. In my conversations with Hispanic/Latino women for this book, a common theme that arose was self-monitoring of their natural self-presentation preferences, to fit in. Many women told me that they avoid wearing vivid colors at work because when they do, their clothing choices are often called out for being "dramatic." Since reactions to women of color vary by their race and ethnicity, the solutions to counter these microaggressions must also be bespoke.

The Secret Lives of Black Women at Work

When Black women get together to commiserate about some of our workplace challenges, it doesn't take long for someone to say, "I told him, you don't have to like me, you just need to respect me." This language has a specific meaning, forged from years of dodging and weaving to make sure our actions "fit in." It is particularly difficult to be a leader when you are "other" than those you lead. It isn't hard to figure out (by reading body language and observing foot-dragging and other delay tactics) when someone who reports to you or with whom you need to collaborate wants to sabotage your efforts. It is, however, all too common.

Invisibility
Isabel Wilkerson is a Pulitzer Prize winner and *New York Times*-bestselling author of two seminal books about the Black experience in America: *The Warmth of Other Suns* and *Caste*. Wilkerson is a bona fide word star! Yet her personal story perfectly illustrates the "invisibility" that Black women face.

While working as a national correspondent for the *New York Times*, Wilkerson showed up at an office for a

Remember that each person
wants nothing more than to
be seen, heard, and valued for
their unique humanity.

pre-arranged interview, but the interviewee refused to meet with her. He told her to leave because, as he put it, "The *New York Times* will be here any minute." The *New York Times* was right in front of him, in the form of Isabel Wilkerson! But he could not see the *New York Times* because he could not see Isabel Wilkerson. Wilkerson remained calm, but I am also sure that she was sobbing on the inside. Despite her laudable self-control, the pain from this infuriating situation was strong enough that she still recounts the experience.

These are not the experiences leaders want for employees. This is the core of the REDI challenge. Black women are often shortchanged, discounted, and rendered invisible by coworkers, clients, and customers. Everybody loses. Think of it this way: when Wilkerson could not do her job, not only did she lose out, but so did her employer, and so did the company that employed the offensive man, since it lost out on priceless coverage in the *New York Times*.

You need to be aware that these dynamics are alive and well and that women of color in your company likely experience these kinds of "checks" regularly. What do we do with these experiences? We do not make a fuss! We don't report it to our managers. Heaven knows we don't report it to HR. Why? We have these experiences so often that if we were to process each one, we would live perpetually in negative emotions. Additionally, we get labeled as "complainers," "victims," or "troublemakers" or of "playing the race card" when we try to broach valid concerns. We are speaking up more now and insisting on parity. Business leaders should listen if you want to uncover the hidden, misunderstood, and underestimated experiences of women of color in your organizations.

What Counters Gender Discrimination at Work?

Dr. W. Brad Johnson and his colleague Dr. David G. Smith have coauthored two books about the experience of women in the workplace. They too found that women of color have different experiences than their White colleagues and are more likely to be marginalized and silenced. In an interview with me, Dr. Johnson offered specific recommendations to support women, particularly women of color, in the workplace.

Support mentoring across races

Mentorships are less likely to form across races because mentors (and mentees) can erroneously believe that cross-race mentoring will not work. This is a fallacy. Mentorship data across several human variations, including gender, race, and sexual orientation, shows that cross-race mentoring relationships are effective. Once established, they move along the same predicable mentoring continuum as other kinds of mentoring. As trust develops, the relationship solidifies. That formation stage is the critical point. Over time the "mere exposure effect" will take over, which means that they will both get more comfortable with each other. Gradually, they will start to really enjoy each other's company, and powerful reciprocal benefits will develop.

Make sponsorship part of the leadership development strategy

Require your leaders, especially senior leaders, to sponsor women so both the sponsor and the person being sponsored see it as an expectation. These expectations minimize awkwardness, too, because all parties will have the same marching orders. Then, track the women's career progress in relation to the sponsorships.

If "culture" is the cake, inclusion is the icing!

Require leaders and employees to act when they see something

Teach leaders and employees to address discrimination in the moment. Dr. Johnson says, "Don't approach the victim 'later' to offer sympathy. Give her your support in the moment," when it is most needed.

Encourage White women to be allies for other women

The nFormation report mentioned earlier revealed that although about 75 percent of White women say they are committed to referring women of color for opportunities and publicly giving us credit for our work, only 29 percent are currently sharing insights with women of color, and only 9 percent are sponsoring a woman of color. Dr. Johnson points out that sometimes people think they are acting as allies when they are not. For example, the intended ally might be friendly to the intended recipient, but that friendliness might not include advocacy or disruption of biased systemic processes. Allyship requires more than friendship!

More about Allyship, Change, and Space for Diverse Voices

Ellen Taaffe is a corporate brand leader turned board director, executive coach, TEDx speaker, and leadership professor at Kellogg School of Management, where she also runs the MBA Women's Leadership program. Ellen interacts with corporate women in all aspects of her work. She believes that organizations can support allies by providing ally groups or other initiatives that enable all employees to advocate for REDI. Microsoft's global Allyship program, for example, is designed to enable all employees to learn the dos and don'ts of effective allyship. "So often people believe in it but don't know how to help. We need allies to become more aware and to learn how they can make a difference," Ellen said in an interview with me.

Ellen also offered other ideas about what works when it comes to countering gender disparities.

Change how you recruit board directors

Ellen says that gender (and racial) diversity is achievable if leaders try new behaviors. "When I have worked to diversify boards from a gender or race perspective, we changed how we recruited directors. We evaluated our needs through a skills matrix to define our criteria. We went to a different source beyond our networks, including registries and recruiting firms. Lastly, we interviewed diverse slates with a consistent interview protocol. If the way we are sourcing talent doesn't yield diverse hires, we have to change our ways."

Purposely enable various opinions (and strengths) to emerge

Ellen recommends that leaders facilitate balanced talktime for all voices and halt behaviors like speaking over and interrupting women and people of color. If someone asks a question in a meeting and it goes unanswered, leaders should note that and circle back (no matter how long that takes) and invite that person to ask their question again. Make room for that woman's perspective!

Create space for open conversations
with unfamiliar employees

Facilitate conversations where women share their experiences of bias with a peer group of both men and women. These sessions can be particularly powerful when senior women share what they experienced when they were at lower levels of the organization and did not have the power they currently possess. Ellen has participated in some of these sessions, and she says, "I saw the shock on the face of men who are their peers now. The men listened, and they will probably never forget what they heard that day. It was a very helpful experience for all involved. So often, people think these issues are ancient history, and they are not." Ellen also notes that these sessions require highly skilled facilitators to provide psychological safety to allay women's concern that their careers could be limited by what they share. Facilitators can be employees who have been trained to specifically moderate these kinds of conversations, but external facilitators are best if employee trust is low in your organization.

As you devise your REDI strategy, pay attention to the unique needs of women of color. Race and gender intersectionality matter!

NOW THAT we have covered the Inclusion MBA model, let's take a step back and think about this challenge as a culture-building opportunity.

I define organizational culture as "what it feels like to work here or do business with the organization." Leaders build culture, and culture drives business performance. A human-centered organizational culture is an ideal foundation for building an inclusive organization. Your culture can be inclusive even if your workforce is not yet as diverse as you want it to be.

EXECUTIVE SUMMARY

- Gender disparities in the workplace are well known, but women of color face a double-whammy when they must deal with the challenges of gender and race simultaneously.

- Women of color are asking for leadership to be redefined. Any such redefinition will benefit not just these women but all employees.

- Organizations will benefit when leaders establish systemic practices, including sponsorship and allyship, to help men and other women understand the experiences of women of color and support their thriving at work.

REDI QUESTIONS

Do you know what women, especially women of color, are experiencing as employees in your organization? What can you do to get clarity about those experiences? What new things could be done in your organization to support these women's career growth and influence? How could the things you do to support women of color benefit all employees?

12

How to Build
a Workplace Culture

. . . .

I N 1995 I was completing my doctoral dissertation and
thinking about my first post-PhD job. I had ruled out academic life. I wanted a corporate job but did not want to
move to the traditional urban centers of commerce—New
York, Chicago, Los Angeles, Atlanta—despite the lure of great
paychecks and big-city glamour. I wanted to live where my
four-year-old daughter could play outside (almost) every day
and where I would see the sun from my office. So, I stayed
in Florida.

I heard that a local company, Raymond James Financial,
Inc. (aka Raymond James), wanted to hire a PhD-level I/O
psychologist. By the time I showed up for my first day, I had
become fascinated by this "little" financial services firm that
did things on its own terms. St. Petersburg, Florida, seemed
like the least likely place for the headquarters of a financial
services company. However, the investment advisory business that Robert A. "Bob" James had started in 1962 was
growing into a full-service financial services company. And

now I had the opportunity to continue my career adventures in this precocious company!

Raymond James turned out to be an ideal employer for me. Over time I built a team and had the chance to regularly advise senior leaders regarding critical talent-selection deci-sions. I found my stride at Raymond James, and many of my colleagues are still friends today. Although I loved working at Raymond James, I didn't fully understand then that my positive day-to-day experience resulted from the intentional efforts of the company leaders to create a human-centered culture. That clarity came years later, as I compared my Ray-mond James history to experiences with other employers.

A Culture of Belonging

Think tank Coqual defines "belonging" as feeling seen, con-nected, supported, and proud. That is how I felt at Raymond James most days and I have never had that experience since then. That is why, although I eventually left the company, it never left me. And I don't take that culture for granted anymore. Over time, I realized that Raymond James was the first place in which I experienced that direct line between effective, professional executive leadership and employee experience.

Raymond James wanted to compete for deals against the behemoths of the financial services world—JPMorgan Chase, Goldman Sachs, Morgan Stanley, and the like. These Wall Street giants had deep pockets and deeper histories. JPMorgan Chase, for example, traces its roots to 1799, while Raymond James was formed 163 years later and did its first underwriting deal in 1969! Somehow, Bob James understood, from the start, that organizational culture could be the great differentiator to power his grandiose ambitions.

That is why the leaders I observed were laser-focused on building a people-focused, values-based culture. They relentlessly drove the expectation that the company's success depended on serving the clients and employees (the company's motto is "Service First"). As it says in the Raymond James principles, "Teamwork and supporting our fellow associates is fundamental to sustaining a work environment that encourages opportunities for unparalleled service, personal growth, and job satisfaction." These ideals were infused into the business operations, using a variety of communication devices, including "Breakfast with the Boss" and "Service First" lunches, where associates could regularly see, talk to, and learn from and with the company's top leaders. Leaders also used these opportunities to celebrate associates' accomplishments and milestones. And Raymond James University made it possible for every associate to develop the knowledge, skills, and behaviors to support "Service First." Eventually, these cultural ambitions were codified in the Raymond James Blueprint, positioning culture as "essential" to the business. This intentional approach partially explains why employees consistently rate the company, its culture, and its CEO very positively in public company reviews.

In addition to founder Bob James, many smart people, including his son Thomas A. "Tom" James, created the Raymond James that I experienced. Bob Shuck, Francis "Bo" Godbold, Larry Silver, Lynn Pippenger, Tom Franke, and Tom Hamilton are among the executives who had their fingerprints on much of my positive experience. Despite the highly competitive nature of capital markets, these leaders pushed Raymond James from "little engine that could" status in 1962, when the father and son started the firm with $20,000, to managing approximately $1.18 trillion in client assets by 2021. The firm currently has almost twenty thousand associates, advisors, and professional partners and has been part of the S&P 500 Index since 2017. This company is a success by any measure. The Raymond James people-first culture has indeed proven to be the company's great competitive advantage.

To find out how it got there, I'm going to do a deep dive on two of those leaders: Tom James (CEO and chairman during my tenure; currently chairman emeritus of RJF, Inc., chairman of Raymond James & Associates, and chairman of Eagle Asset Management) and Bo Godbold (president during my tenure; currently vice-chair of the board of directors of Raymond James Bank). Since these men were involved in building a highly successful business from the ground up, they have a unique perspective on the impact that culture has on business outcomes.

Handcrafted Culture

When I worked at Raymond James, I enjoyed watching how Tom, Bo, and the rest of the leadership team handcrafted the culture daily. Although the company hired some experienced financial services specialists (investment bankers, research analysts, traders, and the like), they were forced to build much of the needed talent capabilities by hiring and training intelligent, people-focused associates with little or no previous financial services experience. Back then, Raymond James could not convince the trained talent from the big Wall Street firms to come to St. Petersburg; the tables have turned!

The first challenge for a CEO who wants to build a human-centered culture is defining the behavioral expectations and holding managers accountable for exhibiting those behaviors.

For several years I led the Assessment and Selection department in HR, managing other I/O psychologists and recruiters who supported the company's efforts to build its talent powerhouse. I spoke with many graduates of excellent schools, including Chicago, Duke, Eckerd College, Florida, Harvard, University of South Florida, University of Tampa, and Wharton. In addition, I interacted with many experienced capital markets professionals from Wall Street financial and trading firms. Raymond James liked to hire talented people who had the "common touch." Each year we conducted rounds of a rigorous assessment process to identify the best talent and screen out the prima donnas and dilettantes. That is part of the secret to how Tom and the other leaders slowly and steadily built a financially successful company and a magnet for world-class talent that routinely outperforms the competition. They don't just hire smart people; they hire *likable* smart people!

One can learn a lot from these leaders' ideas and actions about how **culture impacts business outcomes**. The first challenge for a CEO who wants to build a human-centered culture is defining the behavioral expectations and holding managers accountable for exhibiting those behaviors. Absent this clear definition from the top, employees will not see and feel the difference. You want to set up a culture in which employees remember more positive than negative experiences, like I do about Raymond James.

Neither you nor your organization needs to be perfect today to begin crafting that culture. Start where you are and do the things that can move the needle in the direction you desire. Focus on that every day, and employees will begin to see and feel the difference. The thing that will help most is connecting with employees in ways that let them know you care about them as individuals, whether you are making deals for a global business or a "mom-and-pop" business.

The rest of this chapter culls insights from conversations with Tom James and Bo Godbold. Simply, they are leaders who made me feel they cared. You can have that effect on your employees, too!

Tom James

Tom James's parents may have figured out early on that their son was a financial whiz kid. After all, they watched fifteen-year-old Tom parlay a small loan into a lucrative coin and silver dealership. Tom continued that business while in college, and proceeds from it funded an engagement ring and a honeymoon, which Tom gifted to his beautiful bride. That business also generated income for the young James family in the early 1970s, when Tom was not taking a salary from the firm. He earned money during college booking bands for fraternity and sorority parties and performing as the lead singer!

Tom grew up in a segregated St. Petersburg, but his world-view significantly expanded when he arrived on the Harvard University campus. There, he earned a BA in 1964 and an MBA in 1966. He learned that race, gender, and religion were sometimes used to discriminate against other Americans and, a few years later, resigned from his family's favorite country club when the board refused to accept his nomination of a Jewish friend for membership.

As Tom puts it, "A leader needs a set of beliefs (values) about how you can be successful in an endeavor (and an understanding of what could get in the way). Then you must establish a clear mission, vision, and objectives. And then create mechanisms to enable people in the organization to communicate effectively with one another." In other words, a leader needs to define a North Star that others can use to light their way. Tom started to develop his values-based leadership plan in business school and implemented some of those ideas at Raymond James incrementally. Ever the keen observer, he would read the business context and develop (and write down) the next great idea about how to drive the organization to excel in that context.

I had the good fortune to be in a few meetings with Tom and noticed how he sat back, listening intently to the speaker. Then, he would pepper them with intelligent questions. Woe betide the presenter who could not provide a considered response! But although Tom might destroy a colleague's premise with a few well-timed observations, he was always a teacher, balancing criticism with helpful feedback. These Socratic lessons were just another way to support his long-term vision for a high-growth company.

Whenever I interacted with Tom at the company, he had a kind word, a smile, and sometimes a pep talk. For twenty-five-plus years, I have watched him make "long-run" decisions at Raymond James with the interests of each client and associate in mind. Tom James helped build a people-first culture at Raymond James, in which employees thrive, work well together, and get great things done.

Bo Godbold

A group of MBAs was nervously chatting in a conference room in the Investment Banking department at Raymond James. They checked each other out with tentative sidelong glances even as they puffed out their chests and pranced in their fancy suits, shoes, and briefcases. These young people were future leaders of America and they knew it!

There was always at least one candidate who would behave opposite to the company's people-first values. My evergreen "favorite" is the fellow who dropped names, talked about his pedigree, and refused to answer some of my interview questions. He just couldn't be bothered because, after all, he was sure that he was a "shoo-in." He saw the interview with me as just an annoying formality.

I may have laughed aloud when this fellow bolted from his chair, attempting to end the interview on his own terms, prematurely. Somewhat conspiratorially, the lock on the office door jammed, and he could not dramatically exit as he'd planned! I watched as he fumbled, and when the lock refused to relent, I enjoyed walking past that young man to open the door for him. By that time, his blushing exceeded his bravado.

Tom and Bo had done such a great job defining their cultural expectations that I immediately knew this fellow would not get the job. His behavior did not meet Raymond James' behavior norms. Do you have anyone like this on your team?

After a long morning of interviews like these, I was exhausted. But there were many more to go. Just as I wondered how I could take a bio break, grab lunch, and get back in time for my next interview, Bo Godbold yelled, "Look, Gena, I brought you lunch!" The president of the company was delivering a lunch tray to me! Bo does not remember this moment of typical kindness. But I have never forgotten it.

Bo Godbold joined Raymond James in 1969 when the company was doing a million dollars in revenue. As he points out with his trademark grin, "Today our revenues of about $10 billion a year are ten thousand times more than when I joined!"

Connect with employees in ways that let them know you care about them as individuals, whether you are making deals for a global business or a "mom-and-pop" business.

Bo's upbringing was different from Tom's, yet he became the perfect partner to help build the common-touch culture Raymond James wanted. Bo knew what "good" looked like from a human perspective because his childhood experiences, including being orphaned at age thirteen, had taught him the value of working hard and striving to be self-sufficient. Bo grew up in a segregated South Carolina, but each summer from age thirteen to age eighteen he worked on a crew digging swimming pools; all the members of that crew were Black until Bo joined.

Bo was doing this work in 1950s South Carolina, with its Jim Crow "etiquette," so I was not surprised when he said that initially the crew members did not want to call him by his first name. Bo insisted, and they eventually relented. (By the way, another Raymond James cultural norm is that Tom, Bo, and the other leaders insist that associates call them by their first names. It's a way to reduce an "us" versus "them" mentality and stay connected to all associates.) Over those five summers, Bo and the crew worked together, ate lunch together, used the same restrooms, and traveled in the same vehicle. At that time, people of varying races seldom shared mundane activities like these in the Jim Crow South. Bo and his colleagues developed a mutual respect and worked together to produce excellent results.

Georgia Tech became the first college in the Jim Crow South to voluntarily integrate its student body, in 1961. Bo enrolled that year too, and his classmates included the first three Black students admitted to Tech: Ford C. Greene, Ralph A. Long Jr., and Lawrence M. Williams. In addition, Ronald L. Yancey, the first Black Tech graduate, was part of Bo's graduating class of 1965. Fifty-seven years later, in 2018, Bo and his wife, Betsy, commissioned and funded bronze sculptures to honor these four men. *The Three Pioneers* sculpture, dedicated in September 2019, now stands in Harrison Square at Tech, while the Yancey statue is in Tech's Clough Undergraduate Learning Commons.

Bo Godbold appreciates that humans are more alike than different, an insight that informed his contribution to building the unique Raymond James culture.

Culture Is the Foundation

I included these stories about Tom and Bo to emphasize the criticality of putting culture first when setting up your business expectations.

I am not saying that Raymond James is any less tested than you in dealing with the challenges of operating a successful business in a highly dynamic environment. And, like most businesses, the company continues to work on enhancing diversity. (Interestingly, one of Raymond James' most successful associates is Margaret Starner, whose wealth management practice has over $1 billion in assets under management! In 2020, Margaret won the InvestmentNews Excellence in Diversity, Equity & Inclusion Lifetime Achievement Award, partially because of her contributions to the firm and the industry in fostering opportunities for other women.)

Why am I talking about Raymond James if the company is not perfect? First, after decades of organizational consulting, I have never met a perfect company, and I am not looking for perfection. Second, I differentiate between companies where employees feel like they are part of something big versus those where employees feel simply like a cog in the machinery. Raymond James was the company where I had an unmatched and unforgettable "part of something big," inclusive experience. Third, any company can build an inclusive culture, even if it is still working to enhance the diversity of its workforce. Finally, I think my Raymond James experience illustrates why organizational culture matters not just for employee experience but also business performance.

A healthy organizational culture is a prerequisite and perfect starting point for the REDI journey. You and your company do not need to be perfect. You just need to be willing to learn continuously. Experiment. You'll make mistakes, but employees will have your back as long as you are honest with them. Keep what works; discard the rest. Just keep driving change that employees can see and feel. And, as you do this, your business will thrive, too!

THE LEADERSHIP-FOR-CULTURE TIPS I GLEANED FROM WORKING AT RAYMOND JAMES

- Define cultural expectations first. Then, put mechanisms in place to support execution. Planning is excellent, but execution is the actual test.

- Insist on accountability. State clear expectations and hold leaders accountable for their progress relative to those expectations. Quantify the desired outcomes.

- Nip problems in the bud. Conduct reviews at least twice per year for critical business issues (including REDI work). Once a year is not enough. Don't let problems fester.

EXECUTIVE SUMMARY

- Executive leaders define the culture of the organization.

- Inclusive leadership should be part of the values you build into your organization's culture.

- Employees need to see and feel what you are doing; that is how they judge if your leadership is inclusive or not.

- Whether employees thrive and stay or wither and leave will depend on how they feel about what you build.

REDI QUESTIONS

Do your employees know what you believe about how a positive culture should feel? Do your employees believe that you positively influence the culture of the organization you lead? What behaviors make them think so? What would you have to change for employees to think they are working in an inclusion-oriented organization?

Conclusion

Making Corporate America Better

. . . .

The cause of freedom is not the cause of
a race or a sect, a party or a class—it is the cause
of humankind, the very birthright of humanity.
DR. ANNA JULIA COOPER, *A Voice from the South*

STARTED THIS BOOK with an ambitious goal: to give you
ready access to the deeply personal *and* well-documented
insights of a Black woman and I/O psychologist, gleaned
from twenty-five-plus years studying human behavior
in American corporations. I know my perspective is useful
because executives with whom I have shared this work tell
me they have greater clarity about their role in leading inclusion. They also have a better understanding of what people of
color mean when we say, "Showing up for work is the hardest
thing we do every day."

I hope you have a similar response—the emotions this
book elicits are the most important takeaways! Take time to
let your insights simmer. Once you have explored these ideas
with both your head and your heart, you will see that people
of color need you to help make corporate America less hos-
tile for us. We know that corporate life can be better, and we
know what it would take to make it so. All we ask is that you

partner with us in deriving the solutions that can end this irrational three-tiered system of powerful, less-powerful, and powerless.

Corporate life will never be the same. Ironically, fortuitously, the COVID-19 pandemic changed the rules of the workplace for everyone. This is an ideal time for you to think about rebuilding better. Start with an **Inclusion MBA (Mindset, Boldness, Action)** lens. Add a dose of **"ReEsteemation"** to **build REDI (respect, equity, diversity, and inclusion)** in all aspects of your business. Stop focusing on "the business case for diversity," because what justification is necessary beyond the fact that all humans deserve to be treated fairly and equitably?

The path to this vision of fairness and equity can be tracked and measured via four primary measures:

1 Positive movement on increasing the **representation** of people of color in jobs at all levels in your organization to at least a level of representation that approximates our representation in the available labor force.

2 Positive movement on measures of the **day-to-day experience** of people of color as we interact with our colleagues, clients, and customers, and our access to roles of power and influence.

3 Progress for people of color on **talent access, career mobility, and compensation equity.**

4 Ensuring that **managers are emotionally qualified** and willing to lead people of color with the same respect they offer colleagues of other races—that they are **designated hitters for 100 percent of those they lead.**

Leaders, the bat is yours.

Acknowledgments

. . . .

I AM DEDICATING this book to my beautiful daughter, Marin, hoping it spurs changes that will make the workplace safer for her than it was for me. And to my mother, Clorette; father, Vernon; grandmother Beryl; and grandfather Francis, who have been my secret superpower all along. They helped me feel safe, beautiful, strong, and visible even when the world tried to contradict that view.

Thanks to my partner, Steve, who made space for me to think, insisted that I leave my desk when he could sense that the work was engulfing me, and made our home feel safe.

I would have never written this book without writing coach and publishing strategist AJ Harper. Author and multi-hyphenate Laura Stone's humor and writing tips inspired me often. Dorie Clark has inspired me, since 2014, to take a more intentional approach to living my life's purpose, part of which, I am convinced, is being satisfied by writing this book. Dorie's Recognized Expert community, of which I am a member, inspired, challenged, and supported me. Maya Angelou is the reason I know that my story matters.

Thanks to the folks at Page Two, especially my thoughtful and empathic editors, Kendra Ward and Jenny Govier, genius creative director Peter Cocking, and marketing maven Meghan O'Neill. Special thanks to Trena White, who knows the publishing biz and tells it like it is. Adrineh Der-Boghossian kept me on track.

I interviewed many people for this book, and each was generous with ideas, time, and partnership. Some executives asked to remain anonymous because the book's subject matter is still very sensitive in their organizations. I value their contributions no less than those I can mention here: Alisa Cohn, Andrea Hoffman, April K. Mills, Dr. Calvin Lai, Chris Schembra, Deepa Purushothaman, Dr. Derek R. Avery, Dorie Clark, Ellen Taaffe, Francis "Bo" Godbold, Dr. Kathlyn Wilson, Dr. Kecia Thomas, Lawrence Hamilton, Maria Colacurcio, Dr. Marilyn Gist, Matt Wallaert, Dr. Meisha-ann Martin, Neil Kiefer, Phil Dixon, Ron Carucci, Shellye Archambeau, Thomas A. "Tom" James, Dr. Tiffany Jana, Tom Waterhouse, Tricia Montalvo Timm, and Dr. W. Brad Johnson.

I want to give a shout-out to some relatives, friends, and mentors, some of whom were there from the beginning: my cousin, Sandra Boyce; Trudi Phillips; Doreen Moore; Dr. Gaylene Perrault; Dr. Julius E. Thompson; Dr. Rosemary Closson; Dr. Sandra Thompson; Dr. Walter C. Borman; Daren Pippio; and Lawrence Hamilton.

I am honored and will be eternally grateful to those who endorsed my book. Special thanks to my advance readers whose contributions made the book better.

Thank you all! It takes a village.

Notes

. . . .

Introduction

p. 2   "into Breonna Taylor's apartment, killing her." Heyward, G.,
        & Bogel-Burroughs, N. (2022, February 23). Officer accused of
        recklessly firing in Breonna Taylor raid goes to trial. *The New
        York Times.* nytimes.com/2022/02/23/us/breonna-taylor-brett
        -hankison-trial.html

p. 3   "regardless of their natural human variation." Pope Consulting.
        (2019, December 27). *Dimensions of difference.* popeconsulting
        .com/2019/12/dimensions-of-difference

p. 3   "racial equality is still elusive in broader society." Tomaskovic-
        Devey, D., & McCann, C. (2019). *Who files discrimination
        charges?* Center for Employment Equity, University of
        Massachusetts Amherst. umass.edu/employmentequity/who
        -files-discrimination-charges; Menasce Horowitz, J., Brown,
        A., & Cox, K. (2019, April 9). *Race in America, 2019.* Pew
        Research Center. pewresearch.org/social-trends/2019/04/09/
        race-in-america-2019

p. 3   "the bottom of the workplace hierarchy." Creary, S.J. (2021,
        December). *Beyond promises to progress: Black CEOs and C-suite
        officers speak out on diversity.* Executive Leadership Council.
        elcinfo.com/wp-content/uploads/2021/12/ELC-Beyond
        -Promises-to-Progress.pdf

p. 4   "most Americans still live segregated lives." Menedian, S.,
        Gambhir, S., & Gailes, A. (2021, June 30). *The roots of structural
        racism project: Twenty-first century racial residential segregation in*

249

the United States. Othering & Belonging Institute, University of California, Berkeley. belonging.berkeley.edu/roots-structural -racism; Loh, T.H., Coes, C., & Buthe, B. (2020, December 16). *The great real estate reset: Separate and unequal: Persistent residential segregation is sustaining racial and economic injustice in the US.* Brookings. brookings.edu/essay/trend-1-separate-and -unequal-neighborhoods-are-sustaining-racial-and-economic -injustice-in-the-us

p. 7   "actions that you have seen or experienced)." Sarkis, S. (2017, January 22). 11 red flags of gaslighting in a relationship. *Psychology Today.* psychologytoday.com/us/blog/here-there -and-everywhere/201701/11-warning-signs-gaslighting

p. 7   "like a promotion or pay raise, for example)." Torres, E. (2019, August 12). *Is your boss commitment-phobic?* BBC Worklife. bbc.com/worklife/article/20190723-how-to-tell-if-youre-being -breadcrumbed-at-work

p. 7   "driven by conscious and unconscious bias." Jana, T., & Baran, M. (2020). *Subtle acts of exclusion: How to understand, identify, and stop microaggressions.* Berrett-Koehler.

p. 7   "neither universally experienced nor universally understood." McKinsey & Co. & Lean In. *Women in the workplace 2021.* wiw-report.s3.amazonaws.com/Women_in_the_Workplace_ 2021.pdf

p. 8   "'both a woman question and a race problem.'" Cooper, A.J. (1892 [2000]). *A vision from the South.* [Electronic edition].

p. 8   "that determine power and powerlessness." Crenshaw, K. (2017). *On intersectionality: Essential writings.* New Press.

p. 8   "being stereotyped as 'threatening.'" Reddy, M.T. (1998). Invisibility/hypervisibility: The paradox of normative Whiteness. *Transformations: The Journal of Inclusive Scholarship and Pedagogy, 9*(2), 55–64. jstor.org/stable/43587107

p. 8   "women of any other race or ethnic group." McKinsey & Co. & Lean In. *Women in the workplace 2021.*

Chapter 1: CEOs Can Change America, One Employee at a Time

p. 13   "enslaved Africans in the US of their emancipation." National Museum of African American History and Culture. (2019, June 19). *The historical legacy of Juneteenth.* Smithsonian Institution. nmaahc.si.edu/blog-post/historical-legacy-juneteenth

p. 14   "76 percent White and 13 percent Black." US Census. (n.d.).
        QuickFacts. www.census.gov/quickfacts/fact/table/US/
        PST045219

p. 14   "only about 6 percent are Black." US Bureau of Labor Statistics.
        (2020). *Labor force statistics from the Current Population Survey.*
        bls.gov/cps/cpsaat11.htm

p. 14   "US chief executives are men" Catalyst. (2022, February 9).
        Women in the United States workforce. catalyst.org/research/
        women-in-the-united-states-workforce

p. 15   "their curricula that cover this subject)." Harris, E., & Alter, A.
        (2022, February 8). Book ban efforts spread across the US. *The
        New York Times.* nytimes.com/2022/01/30/books/book-ban
        -us-schools.html

p. 15   "'Black history is American history.'" CBS News. (2006,
        June 14). Freeman on Black history. *60 Minutes.* cbsnews.com/
        video/freeman-on-black-history

p. 16   "not experienced it and don't understand it." Harts, M. (2021).
        Right within: How to heal from racial trauma in the workplace.
        Seal Press; Perry, B.D., & Winfrey, O. (2021). *What happened
        to you? Conversations on trauma, resilience, and healing.* Flatiron
        Books.

p. 16   "the power to change workplaces." Purushothaman, D. (2022).
        *The first, the few, the only: How women of color can redefine power
        in corporate America.* HarperBusiness.

p. 18   "smaller-house neighborhood from the larger houses." Peterman,
        P. (1994, May 8). Down separated streets. *Tampa Bay Times.*
        tampabay.com/archive/1994/05/08/down-separated-streets

p. 18   "by avoiding the tree-named roads." *Atlanta Magazine.*
        (2019, November). Why do street names change at Ponce?
        atlantamagazine.com/list/you-asked-we-answered-34-things
        -you-probably-dont-know-about-atlanta/why-do-street-names
        -change-at-ponce

p. 18   "unless it negatively affects us." National Research Council.
        (2001). *America becoming: Racial trends and their consequences*
        (Vol. 1). National Academies Press.

p. 18   "vary by race and ethnicity." Dunsmuir, L. (2013, August 8).
        Many Americans have no friends of another race: Poll. Reuters.
        reuters.com/article/us-usa-poll-race/many-americans-have-no
        -friends-of-another-race-poll-idUSBRE97704320130808

p. 18   "often starting as early as grade school." Chavez, N. (2021,
        December 5). *Students are fed up with racist slurs and bullying.*

Now they're walking out of class. CNN. cnn.com/2021/12/05/us/racist-bullying-school-incidents/index.html

p. 20   "with my emotional needs in mind." Angelou, M. (1994). Caged bird. From *The complete collection of Maya Angelou.* Random House.

p. 20   "'I Just Wanna Live.'" Bossi, A. (2020, December 21). "I Just Wanna Live" singer Keedron Bryant, 13-year-old behind the viral hit, talks gospel roots and career dreams. *Forbes.* forbes.com/sites/andreabossi/2020/12/21/looking-into-viral -2020-i-just-wanna-live-singer-keedron-bryant-gospel-dreams/ ?sh=200024021b2b

p. 21   "relative to money and time invested." Newkirk, P. (2019). *Diversity, Inc.: The failed promise of a billion-dollar business.* Bold Type Books.

p. 21   "permanent solution to the leaky dyke." Mapes Dodge, M. (1986). *Hans Brinker: Or, the silver skates, a story of life in Holland.* Scribner.

p. 22   "twenty-five years between 1990 and 2015." Quillian, L., Pager, D., Hexel, O., & Midtbøen, A.H. (2017). Meta-analysis of field experiments shows no change in racial discrimination in hiring over time. *Proceedings of the National Academy of Sciences of the United States of America, 114*(41), 10870–10875. doi.org/10.1073/pnas.1706255114

p. 23   "people from traditionally subordinated groups." Apfelbaum, E.P., Norton, M.I., & Sommers, S.R. (2012). Racial color blindness: Emergence, practice, and implications. *Current Directions in Psychological Science, 21*(3), 205–209. doi.org/10.1177/0963721411434980

p. 23   "the risk is perceived to be too great." Tomaskovic-Devey & McCann. *Who files discrimination charges?*

p. 29   "express the emotion of being accepted." Brown, D.L. (2018, August 16). How Aretha Franklin's "Respect" became an anthem for civil rights and feminism. *The Washington Post.* washingtonpost.com/news/retropolis/wp/2018/08/14/how/ -aretha-franklins-respect-became-an-anthem-for-civil-rights -and-feminism

p. 29   "that Black people seek in corporate spaces." Buttny, R., & Williams, P. (2000). Demanding respect: The uses of reported speech in discursive constructions of interracial contact. *Discourse & Society, 11*(1), 109–133. doi.org/10.1177%2F0957926 500011001005

p. 29   "'where we are and where we want to go.'" Putnam-Walkerly,
        K., & Russell, E. (2016, September 15). What the heck does
        "equity" mean? *Stanford Social Innovation Review*. ssir.org/
        articles/entry/what_the_heck_does_equity_mean

p. 30   "not a biological fact." National Human Genome Research
        Institute. (n.d.). *Race.* National Institutes of Health. genome
        .gov/genetics-glossary/Race

p. 31   "Native Hawaiian or Other Pacific Islander." United States
        Census Bureau. (2021, December 3). *About the topic of race.*
        census.gov/topics/population/race/about.html

p. 31   "'language, ancestry, practices, and beliefs.'" APA Style. (2019,
        September). *Race and ethnic identity.* American Psychological
        Association. apastyle.apa.org/style-grammar-guidelines/bias
        -free-language/racial-ethnic-minorities

p. 31   "and Native Americans in this category." You can find an
        explanation for my use of this term by reading this *New York
        Times* article: Wilkerson, I. (2020, July 1). America's enduring
        caste system. *The New York Times.* nytimes.com/2020/07/01/
        magazine/isabel-wilkerson-caste.html

p. 31   "by their specific tribal affiliations." National Museum of
        the American Indian. (n.d.) *Teaching and learning about Native
        Americans.* Smithsonian Institution. americanindian.si.edu/
        nk360/faq/did-you-know

p. 31   "from a continent other than Africa." Adams, C. (2020, June 18).
        Not all Black people are African American. Here's the difference.
        CBS News. cbsnews.com/news/not-all-black-people-are
        -african-american-what-is-the-difference

p. 32   "you will understand why terminology matters." ABC News.
        (2022, February 24). Why Smokey Robinson resents being
        labeled "African American." *The View.* abcnews.go.com/
        theview/video/smokey-robinson-resents-labeled-african
        -american-83091338

p. 32   "in which the words were not capitalized." Mack, K., & Palfrey, J.
        (2020, August 26). Capitalizing Black and White: Grammatical
        justice and equity. MacArthur Foundation. macfound.org/
        press/perspectives/capitalizing-black-and-white-grammatical
        -justice-and-equity

p. 33   "rethinking failure to achieve the goal." Clark, D. (2021). *The
        long game.* Harvard Business Review Press.

p. 33 "the organization's cultural expectations." Cox, G., &
Lancefield, D. (2021, May 19). 5 strategies to infuse D&I into
your organization. *Harvard Business Review.* hbr.org/
2021/05/5-strategies-to-infuse-di-into-your-organization

Chapter 2: Yesterday Explains Today

p. 35 "schools, and workplaces are segregated." Carver, K., & Livers,
A. (2002, November). "Dear White boss..." *Harvard Business
Review.* hbr.org/2002/11/dear-white-boss

p. 35 "are violent criminals, or are not." *Washington Post* staff. (n.d.).
Fatal force. *The Washington Post. PLOS One, 10*(11), Article
e0141854. doi.org/10.1371/journal.pone.0141854; Center for
Policing Equity. (2016, July). *The science of justice: Race, arrests,
and police use of force.* policingequity.org/images/pdfs-doc/CPE_
SoJ_Race-Arrests-UoF_2016-07-08-1130.pdf

p. 35 "tend to split along race lines." DeGue, S., Fowler, K., &
Calkins, C. (2016, November). Deaths due to lethal force by
law enforcement. *American Journal of Preventive Medicine,* 51(5),
S173–187. dx.doi.org/10.1016%2Fj.amepre.2016.08.027

p. 36 "questioning some policing tactics." Graham, D.A. (2021,
May 25). George Floyd's murder changed Americans' views on
policing. *The Atlantic.* theatlantic.com/ideas/archive/2021/05/
george-floyds-murder-changed-how-americans-views-police/
618992

p. 36 "slaves should be 'forever free.'" National Archives Catalog.
(1863). *Emancipation Proclamation.* catalog.archives.gov/id/
299998

p. 37 "and hold public office." Foner, E. (2015, March 28). Why
Reconstruction matters. *The New York Times.* nytimes.com/
2015/03/29/opinion/sunday/why-reconstruction-matters.html

p. 37 "in almost all fifty states." Jim Crow Museum. (n.d.). *The origins
of Jim Crow.* Ferris State University. ferris.edu/htmls/news/
jimcrow/origins.htm; List of Jim Crow law examples by state.
In *Wikipedia.* en.wikipedia.org/wiki/List_of_Jim_Crow_law_
examples_by_state

p. 37 "interracial marriage was criminalized." Solly, M. (2020,
June 4). 158 resources to understand racism in America.
Smithsonian Magazine. smithsonianmag.com/history/158
-resources-understanding-systemic-racism-america-180975029

p. 38 "including travel, education, and transportation." Smithsonian National Museum of American History. (n.d.). Jim Crow laws. americanhistory.si.edu/brown/history/1-segregated/jim -crow.html; Nodjimbadem, K. (2017, May 30). The racial segregation of American cities was anything but accidental. *Smithsonian Magazine.* smithsonianmag.com/history/how -federal-government-intentionally-racially-segregated-american -cities-180963494; Frankenberg, E. (2019, July 19). What school segregation looks like in the US today, in 4 charts. *The Conversation.* theconversation.com/what-school-segregation -looks-like-in-the-us-today-in-4-charts-120061

p. 38 "the completeness of this segregation" Smithsonian National Museum of American History. (n.d.). Separate is not equal. americanhistory.si.edu/brown/history/1-segregated/detail/ jim-crow-laws.html

p. 40 "(a practice known as 'redlining')." US Fair Housing Administration. "Racial" provisions of FHQ Underwriting Manual, 1936. Posted on *Racial and religious covenants in the US and Canada.* wbhsi.net/~wendyplotkin/DeedsWeb/ fha36.html; Stubbs, J.K. (2008, Winter). America's enduring legacy: Segregated housing and segregated schools. Richmond School of Law. commons.trincoll.edu/cssp/2013/09/15/ fha-underwriting-manual; Domonoske, C. (2016, October 19). Interactive redlining map zooms in on America's history of discrimination. *The Two-Way.* NPR. npr.org/sections/thetwo -way/2016/10/19/498536077/interactive-redlining-map-zooms -in-on-americas-history-of-discrimination; Jackson, C. (2021, August 17). What is redlining? *The New York Times.* nytimes .com/2021/08/17/realestate/what-is-redlining.html

p. 40 "are persistent and pernicious." Johns, J., Robinson, L., & Chavez, N. (2021, December 9). *A Black couple had a White friend show their home and its appraisal rose by nearly half a million dollars.* CNN. cnn.com/2021/12/09/business/black -homeowners-appraisal-discrimination-lawsuit/index.html

p. 40 "'separate but equal' unconstitutional." History.com. (2009, October 27). *Brown v. Board of Education.* history.com/topics/ black-history/brown-v-board-of-education-of-topeka

p. 41 "social institutions were deliberately destroyed." Brockell, G. (2021, June 1). Tulsa isn't the only race massacre you were

never taught in school. Here are others. *The Washington Post.*
washingtonpost.com/history/2021/06/01/tulsa-race-massacres
-silence-schools

p. 41   "the enormity of the problem." *Washington Post* staff. (2020,
October 9). Race & reckoning. Resources to understand
America's long history of injustice and inequality. *The
Washington Post.* washingtonpost.com/nation/2020/06/08/
understanding-racism-inequality-america

p. 41   "systemic racism still exists in America." American
Psychological Association. (2012). *Ethnic and racial disparities
in education: Psychology's contribution to understanding and
reducing disparities.* apa.org/ed/resources/racial-disparities;
McIntosh, K., Moss, E., Nunn, R., & Shambaugh, J. (2020,
February 27). *Examining the Black-White wealth gap.* Brookings.
brookings.edu/blog/up-front/2020/02/27/examining-the
-black-white-wealth-gap; Pew Research Center. (2021,
January 12). Racial and ethnic gaps in the US persist on key
demographic indicators. pewresearch.org/interactives/
racial-and-ethnic-gaps-in-the-u-s-persist-on-key-demographic
-indicators; Avery, D.R., & Ruggs, E.N. (2020, July 14).
Confronting the uncomfortable reality of workplace discrimination. *MIT Sloan Management Review.* sloanreview.mit.edu/
article/confronting-the-uncomfortable-reality-of-workplace
-discrimination; Pew Research Center. (2021, August 12). Deep
divisions in Americans' views of national racial history—and
how to address it. pewresearch.org/politics/2021/08/12/deep
-divisions-in-americans-views-of-nations-racial-history-and
-how-to-address-it

p. 42   "'over the past 50 years.'" Peçanha, S. (2020, June 23).
These numbers show that Black and White people live in two
different Americas. *The Washington Post.* washingtonpost.com/
opinions/2020/06/22/what-numbers-say-whites-blacks-live
-two-different-americas

p. 42   "'2 percent of blacks and Hispanics.'" Jan, T. (2017, September
28). White families have nearly 10 times the net worth of
black families. And the gap is growing. *The Washington Post.*
washingtonpost.com/news/wonk/wp/2017/09/28/black-and
-hispanic-families-are-making-more-money-but-they-still-lag
-far-behind-whites

p. 42   "ten times that of Black households." Board of Governors
of the Federal Reserve System. (2017, September 27). *Recent
trends in wealth-holding by race and ethnicity: Evidence from
the Survey of Consumer Finances.* federalreserve.gov/econres/
notes/feds-notes/recent-trends-in-wealth-holding-by-race-and
-ethnicity-evidence-from-the-survey-of-consumer-finances
-20170927.htm

p. 42   "decade between 2010 and 2020." Peçanha, S. These numbers
show that Black and White people live in two different
Americas; National Association of Realtors Research Group.
(2022, February). *A snapshot of race and home buying in America.*
National Association of Realtors.

p. 42   "that of White American infants." National Center for Health
Statistics. (2016). *Health, United States.* Centers for Disease
Control and Prevention. cdc.gov/nchs/hus/contents2016.htm

p. 42   "These disparate health outcomes persisted." Centers for
Disease Control and Prevention. (n.d.). *COVID data tracker:
Demographic trends of COVID-19 cases and deaths in the US
reported to CDC.* covid.cdc.gov/covid-data-tracker/
#demographics

p. 43   "and other economic losses." Snowden, L.R., & Snowden,
J.M. (2021, April). Coronavirus trauma and African Americans'
mental health: Seizing opportunities for transformational
change. *International Journal of Environmental Research Public
Health, 18*(7): 3568. doi.org/10.3390/ijerph18073568; Economic Policy Institute. (2022, March 4). *Economic indicators:
Jobs and unemployment.* epi.org/indicators/unemployment

p. 43   "because of the COVID-19 pandemic." Lean In. (n.d.). *How
COVID-19 is impacting women.*

Chapter 3: The Diversity and Inclusion Imperative

p. 52   "vice president of engineering, told this story." Copeland, R.
(2020, June 26). Google's Marian Croak aimed for the top.
She couldn't escape racism. *The Wall Street Journal.* wsj.com/
articles/googles-marian-croak-aimed-for-the-top-she-couldnt
-escape-racism-11593180017

p. 53   "to make meaningful progress." Cox & Lancefield. 5 strategies
to infuse D&I into your organization.

p. 54   "were represented in their marketing." *AdAge* staff. (2021,
        January 13). A regularly updated blog tracking brands' responses
        to racial injustice. *AdAge.* adage.com/article/cmo-strategy/
        regularly-updated-blog-tracking-brands-responses-racial
        -injustice/2260291

p. 54   "match multiracial skin tones." Milling, M. (2020, June 15).
        Johnson & Johnson announces new Band-Aids, but that can't
        fix racial inequality. *Forbes.* forbes.com/sites/marlamilling/
        2020/06/15/johnson--johnson-announces-new-band-aids-but
        -that-cant-fix-racial-inequality/?sh=6646c34c6e7d

p. 54   "more doors closed than open." Quillian et al. Meta-analysis of
        field experiments shows no change in racial discrimination in
        hiring over time.

p. 56   "their impact on your employees." Jilani, Z. (2019, August
        28). How to beat stereotypes by seeing people as individuals.
        Greater Good Science Center Magazine. greatergood.berkeley
        .edu/article/item/how_to_beat_stereotypes_by_seeing_people_
        as_individuals

p. 56   "hidden, misunderstood, and underestimated." Safdar, K., &
        Hagey, K. (2020, June 26). Black executives are sharing their
        experiences of racism, many for the first time. *The Wall Street
        Journal.* wsj.com/articles/black-executives-are-sharing-their
        -experiences-of-racism-many-for-the-first-time-11593182200

p. 57   "the 'invisibility paradox.'" Smith, A.N., Baskerville Watkins,
        M., Ladge, J., & Carlton, P. (2019, December 19). Making the
        invisible visible: Paradoxical effects of intersectional invisibility
        on the career experiences of executive Black women. *Academy
        of Management Journal, 62*(6). doi.org/10.5465/amj.2017.1513

p. 58   "outcomes among African Americans." Williams, D.R., &
        Williams-Morris, R. (2000). Racism and mental health: The
        African American experience. *Ethnicity and Health, 5*(3/4),
        243–268. doi.org/10.1080/713667453

p. 58   "People of Color and Indigenous individuals (POCI)." Comas-
        Díaz, L., Hall, G.N., & Neville, H.A. (2019). Racial trauma:
        Theory, research, and healing: Introduction to the special
        issue. *American Psychologist, 74*(1), 1–5. dx.doi.org/10.1037/
        amp0000442

p. 58   "real or perceived experiences of racial discrimination." Carter,
        R.T. (2007, January). Racism and psychological and emotional
        injury: Recognizing and assessing race-based traumatic stress.

The Counseling Psychologist, 35(1), 13–105. doi.org/10.1177%
2F0011000006292033

p. 59 "insights in the Edelman Trust Barometer." Edelman. (2021).
Edelman Trust Barometer 2021. edelman.com/sites/g/files/
aatuss191/files/2021-01/2021-edelman-trust-barometer.pdf

p. 59 "non-governmental organizations, and media declined."
Edelman. (2022). *2022 Edelman Trust Barometer.* edelman.com/
trust/2022-trust-barometer

p. 60 "balance profit with common good." Department of Economic
and Social Affairs Sustainable Development. (n.d.). *The 17 Goals.*
United Nations. sdgs.un.org/goals

p. 60 "unless leaders step up to fix it." Hatzipanagos, R. (2021,
March 15). Gen Z is making change, one protest at a time.
The Washington Post. washingtonpost.com/nation/2021/03/15/
gen-z-is-making-change-one-protest-time; Echelon Insights &
Walton Family Foundation. (2021). *Millennials and Generation
Z: Agents of change.* waltonfamilyfoundation.org/learning/
millennials-and-generation-z-agents-of-change

p. 60 "'other members of that community.'" Fukuyama, F. (1995).
Trust: The social virtues and the creation of prosperity. Free Press.

p. 60 "'they do the right thing.'" Edelman. (2021). *20 years of trust.*
edelman.com/20yearsoftrust

p. 60 "'to persist across the world.'" Department of Economic and
Social Affairs Sustainable Development. (2020). *SDG #10:
Reduced inequalities.* United Nations. un.org/sustainable
development/wp-content/uploads/2018/01/10_Why-It
-Matters-2020.pdf

p. 61 "some of America's largest companies." Business Roundtable.
(n.d.). *About us.* businessroundtable.org/about-us

p. 61 "'that serves all Americans.'" Business Roundtable. (2019,
August 19). *Business Roundtable redefines the purpose of a
corporation to promote "an economy that serves all Americans."*
businessroundtable.org/business-roundtable-redefines-the
-purpose-of-a-corporation-to-promote-an-economy-that-serves
-all-americans

p. 61 "emerged from Milton Friedman's writings." Friedman, M.
(1970, September 13). A Friedman doctrine: The social
responsibility of business is to increase its profits. *The New
York Times.* nytimes.com/1970/09/13/archives/a-friedman
-doctrine-the-social-responsibility-of-business-is-to.html

p. 61   "Advance Racial Equity and Justice." Business Roundtable. (n.d.).
        Advancing racial equity and justice. businessroundtable.org/equity

p. 62   "diversity and inclusion in the workplace." CEO Action for
        Diversity & Inclusion. (n.d.). *FAQs.* ceoaction.com/faqs

p. 62   "'extraordinary change is possible.'" Samuelson, J. (2021).
        The six new rules of business: Creating value in a changing world.
        Berrett-Koehler.

p. 62   "ethnically diverse than any other." Parker, K., & Igielnik, R.
        (2020, May 14). *On the cusp of adulthood and facing an uncertain
        future: What we know about Gen Z so far.* Pew Research Center.
        pewresearch.org/social-trends/2020/05/14/on-the-cusp-of
        -adulthood-and-facing-an-uncertain-future-what-we-know
        -about-gen-z-so-far-2

p. 62   "ethics and social impact." Deloitte. (n.d.). *Understanding
        Generation Z in the workplace.* www2.deloitte.com/us/en/pages/
        consumer-business/articles/understanding-generation-z-in
        -the-workplace.html

p. 62   "above environment and social change." Blue Shield of
        California. (2021, April 15). *Gen Z youth say climate change is
        adversely affecting their physical and mental health in new national
        survey by Blue Shield of California.* news.blueshieldca.com/
        2021/04/15/NextGenGoals; Gilbert, A. (2021, April 21).
        Climate change, racism, and social justice concerns affecting
        Gen Z's physical and mental Health. *USA Today.* usatoday.com/
        story/life/2021/04/21/climate-change-racism-and-social
        -justice-major-concerns-gen-z/7289512002

p. 62   "'we can start a movement.'" Cohen, L. (2020, July 20). *From
        TikTok to Black Lives Matter, how Gen Z is revolutionizing
        activism.* CBS News. cbsnews.com/news/from-tiktok-to-black
        -lives-matter-how-gen-z-is-revolutionizing-activism

p. 63   "by ethnic or racial group." Glassdoor. (2020, September).
        Diversity & Inclusion Workplace Survey. b2b-assets.glassdoor
        .com/glassdoor-diversity-inclusion-workplace-survey.pdf

p. 63   "about prejudice and discrimination." Edelman. *2022 Edelman
        Trust Barometer.*

p. 65   "European Union leading the charge." European Union. (n.d.).
        Sustainable finance. ec.europa.eu/info/business-economy-euro/
        banking-and-finance/sustainable-finance_en

p. 65   "public stance for disclosure." Vaghul, K. (2021, January 19).
        A small fraction of corporations shares diversity data, but disclosure

is rapidly on the rise. JUST Capital. justcapital.com/reports/
share-of-largest-us-companies-disclosing-race-and-ethnicity
-data-rises

p. 65   "Civil Rights Act of 1964." US Equal Employment Opportunity
Commission. (n.d.). *EEO-1 data collection.* eeoc.gov/employers/
eeo-1-data-collection

p. 65   "reported on the EEO-1." Vaghul, K., Ira, K., Radeva, A., &
Caro, C. (n.d.). *Beyond demographic data disclosure: The state
of gender and racial representation at America's largest companies.*
JUST Capital. justcapital.com/reports/beyond-demographic
-data-disclosure-the-state-of-gender-and-racial-representation
-at-americas-largest-companies

p. 65   "evolving environmental and social realities." JUST Capital.
(n.d.). *Survey analysis: Two years later, do Americans believe
companies are living up to the Business Roundtable's redefined
Purpose of a Corporation?* justcapital.com/reports/do-americans
-believe-companies-are-living-up-to-business-roundtables
-purpose-of-a-corporation-2021

p. 66   "to meeting those targets." McDonald's. (n.d.). *Diversity, equity
& inclusion.* corporate.mcdonalds.com/corpmcd/our-purpose
-and-impact/jobs-inclusion-and-empowerment/diversity-and
-inclusion.html

p. 66   "'inclusion within the Company.'" McDonald's. (2021, February
18). *Allyship through accountability.* corporate.mcdonalds.com/
corpmcd/en-us/our-stories/article/press-releases.global-dei
-ambition.html

p. 66   "diversity and inclusion outcomes." Starbucks. (2020,
October 14). *Our commitment to inclusion, diversity, and
equity at Starbucks.* stories.starbucks.com/stories/2020/
our-commitment-to-inclusion-diversity-and-equity-at-starbucks

p. 66   "bisexual, transgender, or queer." Osipovich, A. (2021, August
6). Nasdaq's board-diversity proposal wins SEC approval. *The
Wall Street Journal.* wsj.com/articles/nasdaqs-board-diversity
-proposal-faces-sec-decision-11628242202

p. 66   "challenging this Nasdaq rule." Alliance for Fair Board
Recruitment and National Center for Public Policy Research v.
Securities and Exchange Commission. Case 21-60626. (5th Cir
2021). Amicus Brief of the States of… texasattorneygeneral
.gov/sites/default/files/images/executive-management/NAS
DAQ%20SEC%20CA5%20State%20Amicus%20Br%20Filed.pdf

Chapter 4: Understand Your Beliefs about REDI

p. 72   "alienating and disengaging behavior." Carver & Livers, "Dear White boss..."

p. 72   "terms are often used interchangeably." American Psychological Association. (n.d.). Anxiety. *APA Dictionary of Psychology.* dictionary.apa.org/anxiety

p. 73   "racial justice, in the workplace." Barber, G. (2020, October 15). The turmoil over "Black Lives Matter" and political speech at Coinbase. *Wired.* wired.com/story/turmoil-black-lives-matter -political-speech-coinbase

p. 73   "speak out publicly about these issues." Murray, A., & Meyer, D. (2021, May 18). Should CEOs speak out about controversial social and political issues? *Fortune.* fortune.com/2021/05/18/ should-ceos-speak-out-about-controversial-social-and-political -issues-stakeholder-capitalism-ceo-daily

p. 73   "'taken out of context by the media.'" Thompson, D. (2020, July 29). *Scared to talk about race, diversity, equity and inclusion? Here's how to start.* WRAL TechWire. wraltechwire.com/2020/ 07/29/scared-to-talk-about-race-diversity-equity-and-inclusion -heres-how-to-start

p. 73   "action to address race-based disparities." Hartmann, D. (2012, March 1). *Happy talk about diversity avoids difficult racial issues.* Scholars Strategy Network. scholars.org/brief/ happy-talk-about-diversity-avoids-difficult-racial-issues

p. 74   "competencies (actions) of inclusive leaders." Tapia, A., & Polonskaia, A. (2020). *The 5 disciplines of inclusive leaders: Unleashing the power of all of us.* Berrett-Koehler.

p. 75   "concept of 'growth mindset.'" Dweck, C. (2016, January 13). What having a "growth mindset" actually means. *Harvard Business Review.* hbr.org/2016/01/what-having-a-growth -mindset-actually-means

p. 75   "'novel solutions to new and old problems.'" O'Keefe, P.A., Dweck, C.S., & Walton, G.M. Implicit theories of interest: Finding your passion or developing it? *Psychological Science, 29* (10), 1653–1664. doi.org/10.1177%2F0956797618780643

p. 76   "perpetrators believe they are not prejudiced." Dovidio, J., Gaertner, S., Kawakami, K., & Hodson, G. Why can't we just get along? Interpersonal biases and interracial distrust. *Cultural Diversity & Ethnic Minority Psychology, 8*(2), 88–102. doi.org/ 10.1037/1099-9809.8.2.88

p. 78　"coauthored with Jason Greer." Greer, J., & Dixon, P. *Bias, racism and the brain: How we got here and what needs to happen next.* OBI Press.

p. 78　"ready to respond, but more slowly." Dixon, P. (2020, December 21; 2021, January 15). Personal communication.

p. 80　"'to eliminate our biases...'" Morse, G. (2016, July–August). Designing a bias-free organization. *Harvard Business Review.* hbr.org/2016/07/designing-a-bias-free-organization

p. 82　"that discolor what we 'see.'" Escalante, V. (2022, February 2). Personal communication.

p. 82　"are not the same thing." Payne, B.K., & Hannay, J.W. (2021, November). Implicit bias reflects systemic racism. *Trends in Cognitive Sciences, 25*(11), P927–936. doi.org/10.1016/j.tics.2021.08.001

p. 83　"criminals in mainstream movies and media." National Museum of African American History and Culture. (n.d.). *Being antiracist.* Smithsonian. nmaahc.si.edu/learn/talking-about-race/topics/being-antiracist

p. 83　"'despite the presence of group-based inequality.'" Rucker, J.M., & Richeson, J.A. (2021, October 14). Toward an understanding of structural racism: Implications for criminal justice. *Science, 374*(6565), 286–290. science.org/doi/epdf/10.1126/science.abj7779

p. 83　"debate about Critical Race Theory is a case in point." Fortin, J. (2021, November 8). Critical race theory: A brief history. *The New York Times.* nytimes.com/article/what-is-critical-race-theory.html

p. 83　"White Americans focus more on interpersonal bias." Pew Research Center. (2016, June 24). *How Blacks and Whites view the state of race in America.* pewresearch.org/social-trends/interactives/state-of-race-in-america

p. 86　"race or ethnic group other than their own." Wilson, K. (2021, September 7). Personal communication.

p. 86　"redesigned its performance management system years ago." Buckingham, M., & Goodall, A. (2015, April). Reinventing performance management. *Harvard Business Review.* hbr.org/2015/04/reinventing-performance-management

p. 87　"'opposite of what they say they want to do!'" Wallaert, M. (2020, December 20). Personal communication.

p. 88   " 'Why does this matter to you personally?' " Johnson, W.B. (2021, February 12 & 26). Personal communication.

p. 92   "you are not alone." Auger-Dominguez, D. (2019, November 8). Getting over your fear of talking about diversity. *Harvard Business Review*. hbr.org/2019/11/getting-over-your-fear-of-talking-about-diversity; National Museum of African American History and Culture, *Being antiracist*; Rucker & Richeson, Toward an understanding of structural racism; Pew Research Center, *How Blacks and Whites view the state of race in America*.

p. 93   "engaged and inspired at work." The HOW Institute for Society. (2021, March). *Human connection in the virtual workplace.* thehowinstitute.org/wp-content/uploads/2021/03/HOW_Institute_Human_Connection_Report_spread.pdf

p. 93   "influence on employee experience." Beck, R.J., & Harter, J. (n.d.). *Why great managers are so rare*. Gallup. gallup.com/workplace/231593/why-great-managers-rare.aspx

p. 94   "their frame of reference rather than one's own." American Psychological Association. (n.d.). Empathy. *APA Dictionary of Psychology*. dictionary.apa.org/empathy

p. 94   "understanding that drives business outcomes." Wade, A.S. (2022). *Empathy works: The key to competitive advantage in the new era of work*. Page Two.

p. 94   "were targeted by bomb threats!" Lampen, C. (2022, February 3). *What we know about the bomb threats at HBCUs*. The Cut. thecut.com/2022/02/hbcu-bomb-threats-everything-we-know-so-far.html

p. 95   "but she says it is doable." Cohn, A. (2021, January 15). Personal communication.

p. 95   "credibility when they ask questions!" Cojuharenco, I., & Karelaia, N. (2020). When leaders ask questions: Can humility premiums buffer the effects of competence penalties? *Organizational Behavior and Human Decision Processes*, *156*, 113-134. doi.org/10.1016/j.obhdp.2019.12.001

p. 95   "conversations between strangers can be highly satisfying." Kardas, M., Kumar, A., & Epley, N. (2022). Overly shallow? Miscalibrated expectations create a barrier to deeper conversation. *Journal of Personality and Social Psychology*, *122*(3), 367-398. dx.doi.org/10.1037/pspa0000281

p. 96   "they are transformed." Montalvo Timm, T. (2021, May 26). Personal communication.

p. 96   " 'payoff for building both is significant!' " Clark, D. (2021, January 14). Personal communication.

p. 96   "foundation for all strong connections and relationships." Schembra, C. (2021, February 23). Personal communication.

p. 97   "can be useful conversation starters." #CultureTags: culturetags.com/pages/about; So Cards: socards.org/about; Over Coffee: overcoffeegames.com; Cards for Connection: gamesforhumanity.com/collections/games/products/cards -for-connection®-deck

p. 100   "race and ethnicity groupings are more complex—and contentious." Mistlin, A. (2021, April 8). So the term BAME has had its day. But what should replace it? *The Guardian.* theguardian.com/commentisfree/2021/apr/08/bame-britain -ethnic-minorities-acronym

p. 101   "Lawrence advises." Hamilton, L. (2021, July 8). Personal communication.

p. 101   "higher standard of integrity than before." Carucci, R. (2021, February 8). Personal communication.

p. 101   " 'block others from also choosing the change.' " Mills, A.K. (2021). *Change tactics: 50 ways change agents boldly escape the status quo.* Engine for Change Press.

Chapter 5: The Truth about Working in Your Organization

p. 107   "candor and vulnerability are welcome." Edmondson, A.C., & Hugander, P. (2021, June 22). 4 steps to boost psychological safety at your workplace. *Harvard Business Review.* hbr.org/ 2021/06/4-steps-to-boost-psychological-safety-at-your -workplace

p. 107   "listen more than you tell." Gregersen, H. (2017, March–April). Bursting the CEO bubble. *Harvard Business Review.* hbr.org/ 2017/03/bursting-the-ceo-bubble

p. 107   "give them the microphone." Reitz, M., & Higgins, J. (2019, July 18). Managers, you're more intimidating than you think. *Harvard Business Review.* hbr.org/2019/07/managers-youre -more-intimidating-than-you-think

p. 107   "searching for new top executives." Fitzgerald, J. (2021, October 26). *What companies want most in a CEO: A good listener.* Harvard Business School Working Knowledge. hbswk.hbs.edu/ item/what-companies-want-most-in-a-ceo-a-good-listener

p. 108 "threw a basketball to each other." Simons, D.J., & Chabris, C.F. (1999). Gorillas in our midst: Sustained inattentional blindness for dynamic events. *Perception, 28*(9), 1059–1074. doi.org/ 10.1068/p281059

p. 108 "'we're actually missing a whole lot.'" Chabris, C., & Simons, D. (2011). *The invisible gorilla: How our intuitions deceive us.* Harmony.

p. 108 "Kilivila language of Papua New Guinea." Carucci, R., & Hansen, E. (2014). *Rising to power: The journey of exceptional executives.* Greenleaf Book Group.

p. 110 "leaders get their college educations." Dvorak, P. (2007, February 12). MBA programs hone "soft skills." *The Wall Street Journal.* wsj.com/articles/SB117124443482305364

p. 110 "underemphasized in business schools." Wilkie, D. (2019, October 21). *Employers say students aren't learning soft skills in college.* Society for Human Resource Management. shrm.org/resourcesandtools/hr-topics/employee-relations/ pages/employers-say-students-arent-learning-soft-skills-in -college.aspx

p. 110 "'a certain kind of person.'" Kolditz, T., Gill, L., & Brown, R. (2020). *Leadership reckoning: Can higher education develop the leaders we need?* Monocle Press.

p. 110 "elevate leadership development across the nation." Franklin, A.R. (2022, February 28). *Doerr Institute spearheads efforts to develop leaders across the country.* Office of Public Affairs News and Media Relations, Rice University. news.rice.edu/news/ 2022/doerr-institute-spearheads-efforts-develop-leaders -across-country

p. 111 "'It's okay not to have a perfect story.'" *Washington Post* Live. (2021, April 15). Race in America: Corporate leadership with PwC US chair & senior partner Tim Ryan. *The Washington Post.* washingtonpost.com/washington-post-live/2021/04/15/race -america-corporate-leadership-with-pwc-us-chair-senior-partner -tim-ryan

p. 111 "'no less likely to discriminate.'" Livingston, R. (2020, September–October). How to promote racial equity in the workplace. *Harvard Business Review.* hbr.org/2020/09/how-to -promote-racial-equity-in-the-workplace

p. 111 "support authenticity and new forms of power." nFormation & Billie Jean King Leadership Initiative. (2021). *PowHER*

Redefined: Women of Color Reimagining the World of Work.
powherredefined.com

p. 113 "'not living up to those commitments.'" Haddon, H. (2021, March 13). Starbucks's Mellody Hobson, the only Black chairwoman in S&P 500, says "Civil Rights 3.0" is brewing. *The Wall Street Journal.* wsj.com/articles/starbuckss-mellody -hobson-the-only-black-chairwoman-in-s-p-500-says-civil -rights-3-0-is-brewing-11615651200

p. 113 "Black experience in corporate America." Cox & Lancefield, 5 strategies to infuse D&I into your organization.

p. 116 "greatest impact on the day-to-day experience of employees." Beck, R., & Harter, J. (2015, April 21). *Managers account for 70% of variance in employee engagement.* Gallup. news.gallup.com/ businessjournal/182792/managers-account-variance-employee -engagement.aspx

Chapter 6: CEO and Board Using the Same Playbook

p. 122 "'Where were you?'" Taylor, K. (2020, October 14). Corporate board members demand refunds and threaten to "rage quit" after writer Anand Giridharadas lambasts them in a virtual conference. *Business Insider.* businessinsider.com/writer-anand -giridharadas-slams-corporate-directors-2020-10

p. 122 "'redefine how businesses create value.'" Ibid.

p. 123 "target opportunities and confront challenges." Moyo, D. (2021). *How boards work: And how they can work better in a chaotic world.* Basic Books.

p. 124 "'deliberately rigged against ethnic minorities.'" Commission on Race and Ethnic Disparities. (2021, March). *The report.* assets.publishing.service.gov.uk/government/uploads/system/ uploads/attachment_data/file/974507/20210331_-_CRED_ Report_-_FINAL_-_Web_Accessible.pdf

p. 124 "CRED conclusions and recommendations." Kaur, R., & Hague, G.M. (2021, April 1). Race commission report: The rights and wrongs. *The Conversation.* theconversation.com/race-commission -report-the-rights-and-wrongs-158316

p. 126 "'always requires constant attention.'" Fubini, D. (2020). *Hidden truths: What leaders need to hear but are rarely told.* Wiley.

p. 126 "nudged into embracing the idea." Samuelson. *The six new rules of business.*

p. 126   "boards of most US companies are not diverse." Buck, M., & Crawford, V. (2021, June 23). It's time to make board diversity an expectation, not just a priority. *Fortune.* fortune.com/2021/06/23/board-diversity-women-poc-inclusion-talent-business-leadership

p. 127   "particularly in business settings." Williams, E.K. (2020, June 16). Yes, you must talk about race at work: 3 ways to get started. *Forbes.* forbes.com/sites/ebonikwilliams/2020/06/16/yes-you-must-talk-about-race-at-work-3-ways-to-get-started

p. 127   "'comfortable' in dealing with race." Bergner, G. (2009). *Taboo subjects: Race, sex, and psychoanalysis.* University of Minnesota Press.

p. 128   "corporate board decision making and employee experience." Palladino, L. (2021). Economic democracy at work: Why (and how) workers should be represented on US corporate boards. *Journal of Law and Political Economy, 1*(3). dx.doi.org/10.5070/LP61353763

p. 129   "impact most interpersonal and group outcomes." Groysberg, B., Lee, J., Price, J., & Yo-Jud Cheng, J. (2018, January–February). The leader's guide to corporate culture. *Harvard Business Review.* hbr.org/2018/01/the-leaders-guide-to-corporate-culture

p. 129   "board's culture and the larger organization interact." Ibid.

p. 131   "that role is rising." National Association of Corporate Directors. (2010). *Role of the lead director.* nacdonline.org/files/PDF/NACD-%20Role%20of%20the%20Lead%20Director_1284573862798.pdf

p. 131   "you will focus on in this work." Pope Consulting, *Dimensions of difference.*

p. 132   "lowest belonging scores among all women." Achievers Workforce Institute. (2021). *Belonging at work: 2021 culture report.* achievers.com/wp-content/uploads/2021/08/Achievers-Workforce-Institute_2021-Culture-Report_Belonging-at-Work.pdf

p. 132   "never interacted with a senior leader in their organization!" Lean In. (n.d.). *The state of Black women in corporate America.* media.sgff.io/sgff_r1eHetbDYb/2020-08-13/1597343917539/Lean_In_-_State_of_Black_Women_in_Corporate_America_Report_1.pdf

p. 132   "*Missing Pieces* report in June 2021." Deloitte & Alliance for Board Diversity. (2021). *Missing pieces report: The board diversity census of women and minorities on Fortune 500 boards*

(6th ed.). www2.deloitte.com/us/en/pages/center-for-board
-effectiveness/articles/missing-pieces-board-diversity-census
-fortune-500-sixth-edition.html

p. 133   "are underrepresented on boards." US Census, *QuickFacts*.

p. 133   "Black and Latino directors on their boards." Francis, T., &
Maloney, J. (2021, June 16). Big companies boost share of Black
and Latino directors. *The Wall Street Journal*. wsj.com/articles/
this-years-influx-of-directors-starts-shift-in-boardroom
-diversity-11623835801#comments_sector

p. 133   "characteristics influence their perspectives." Russell Reynolds
Associates. (2017). *Different is better: Why diversity matters
in the boardroom*. orgwise.ca/sites/osi.ocasi.org.stage/files/
Diversity%20on%20the%20Board.pdf

p. 133   "'more positive satisfaction levels.'" Creek, S., Kuhn, K., &
Sahaym, A. (2019). Board diversity and employee satisfaction:
The mediating role of progressive programs. *Group &
Organization Management, 44*(3), 521–548. doi.org/10.1177/
1059601117740498

p. 134   "'with fewer unforced errors.'" Archambeau, S. (2020,
November 4). Personal communication.

p. 134   "'growth and potential of entrepreneurs of color.'" Nasdaq.
(n.d.). *Inclusive entrepreneurship*. nasdaq.com/inclusive
-entrepreneurship

p. 135   "opinion piece by Arthur Levitt Jr." Levitt Jr., A. (2021, January
20). If corporate diversity works, show me the money. *The Wall
Street Journal*. wsj.com/articles/if-corporate-diversity-works
-show-me-the-money-11611183633

p. 136   "won SEC approval in August 2021." Nasdaq. (2021, October 1).
*Nasdaq's Board Diversity Rule: What Nasdaq-listed companies
should know*. listingcenter.nasdaq.com/assets/Board%20
Diversity%20Disclosure%20Five%20Things.pdf

p. 138   "'and greater relative profits.'" Herring, C. (2009, April). Does
diversity pay? Race, gender, and the business case for diversity.
American Sociological Review, 74(2), 208–224. doi.org/10.117
7%2F000312240907400203

p. 138   "neurodiverse and LGBTQ+-supportive." Austin, R.D., &
Pisano, G.P. (2017, May–June). Neurodiversity as a competitive
advantage. *Harvard Business Review*. hbr.org/2017/05/neuro
diversity-as-a-competitive-advantage; Badgett, M.V.L., Durso,
L.E., Kastanis, A., & Mallory, C. (2013, May). *The business*

impact of LGBT-supportive workplace policies. UCLA School
of Law Williams Institute. williamsinstitute.law.ucla.edu/
publications/impact-lgbt-supportive-workplaces

Chapter 7: The C-Suite Inclusion Infusion

p. 143 "50 percent of leaders and managers might not naturally
support REDI matters." Chudy, J., & Jefferson, H. (2021, May
22). Support for Black Lives Matter surged last year. Did it
last? *The New York Times.* nytimes.com/2021/05/22/opinion/
blm-movement-protests-support.html

p. 146 "yield unique REDI patterns." Martin, R.L., & Riel, J. (2019,
July–August). The one thing you need to know about managing
functions. *Harvard Business Review.* hbr.org/2019/07/the-one
-thing-you-need-to-know-about-managing-functions

p. 146 "Neutral and Inferior Instrument model." Golembiewski,
R.T. (1961, August). Toward the new organization theories:
Some notes on "staff." *Midwest Journal of Political Science,*
5(3), 237–259. doi.org/10.2307/2108937

p. 146 "alternative organizational structures to this line/staff
arrangement." Hirschhorn, L., & Gilmore, T. (1992, May–June).
The new boundaries of the "boundaryless" company. *Harvard
Business Review.* hbr.org/1992/05/the-new-boundaries-of-the
-boundaryless-company

p. 146 "client-facing/non-client-facing distinctions persist." Bernstein,
E., Bunch, J., Canner, N., & Lee, M.Y. (2016, July–August).
Beyond the holacracy hype. *Harvard Business Review.* hbr.org/
2016/07/beyond-the-holacracy-hype

p. 147 "and revenue-generating authority." US Bureau of Labor Statistics,
Labor force statistics from the Current Population Survey.

p. 147 "'simply because they work in the wrong place.'" Ingram, P.
(2021, January–February). The forgotten dimension of diversity.
Harvard Business Review. hbr.org/2021/01/the-forgotten
-dimension-of-diversity

p. 148 "'there are relatively few of them there.'" The Upshot. (2017,
January 18). Some colleges have more students from the top
1 percent than the bottom 60. *The New York Times.* nytimes
.com/interactive/2017/01/18/upshot/some-colleges-have-more
-students-from-the-top-1-percent-than-the-bottom-60.html

p. 148 "than the so-called 'elite' schools." Leonhardt, D. (2017,
January 18). American's great working-class colleges.

The New York Times. nytimes.com/2017/01/18/opinion/sunday/
americas-great-working-class-colleges.html

p. 149 "exacerbated by the COVID-19 pandemic." Auginbaugh, A., &
Rothstein, D.S. (2022, January). How did employment change
during the COVID-19 pandemic? Evidence from a new BLS
survey supplement. US Bureau of Labor Statistics. *Beyond the
Numbers, 11*(1). www.bls.gov/opub/btn/volume-11/how-did
-employment-change-during-the-covid-19-pandemic.htm

p. 150 "more than sixty US companies hired their first-ever CDO." Cox
& Lancefield, 5 strategies to infuse D&I into your organization.

p. 150 "in response to the Civil Rights movement." Vaughn, B. (2007).
Managing diversity: The history of diversity training & its
pioneers. *Diversity Officer Magazine.* diversityofficermagazine
.com/cultural-diversity-factoids/historical-issues

p. 150 "violating federal civil rights laws." US Equal Employment
Opportunity Commission. (n.d.). *Laws enforced by EEOC.*
eeoc.gov/statutes/laws-enforced-eeoc

p. 150 "unconscious bias awareness." Kalev, A., & Dobbin, F. (2020,
October 20). Companies need to think bigger than diversity
training. *Harvard Business Review.* hbr.org/2020/10/
companies-need-to-think-bigger-than-diversity-training

p. 150 "product and service design and delivery." Mallick, M. (2020,
September 11). Do you know why your company needs a Chief
Diversity Officer? *Harvard Business Review.* hbr.org/2020/09/
do-you-know-why-your-company-needs-a-chief-diversity-officer

p. 152 "may create unintended disruption." Lancefield, D. (2021,
November 22). Mastering the connection between strategy
and culture. *Strategy + Business.* strategy-business.com/article/
Mastering-the-connection-between-strategy-and-culture

p. 153 "when it comes to REDI?" Collins, J., & Porras, J.I. (1996,
September–October). Building your company's vision.
Harvard Business Review. hbr.org/1996/09/building-your
-companys-vision

p. 155 "'tie leader bonuses to these outcomes.'" Hoffman, A. (2020,
November 30). Personal communication.

p. 157 "address collective choice problems." IGI Global. (n.d.). What
is coordination mechanism. *InfoSci-Dictionary.* igi-global.com/
dictionary/coordination-mechanism/5892

Chapter 8: A CDO with Resources and Political Clout

p. 164   "turnover among CDOs has *also* increased?" Green, J.
(2021, March 12). Help wanted: Diversity officer hiring is
booming in the US. *Bloomberg News.* bloomberg.com/news/
articles/2021-03-12/help-wanted-diversiy-officer-hiring-is
-booming-in-the-u-s; Cutter, C., & Weber, L. (2020, July 13).
Demand for Chief Diversity Officers is high. So is turnover.
The Wall Street Journal. wsj.com/articles/demand-for-chief
-diversity-officers-is-high-so-is-turnover-11594638000

p. 164   "necessary to make REDI changes." Jan, T. (2021, December 15).
The striking race gap in corporate America. *The Washington
Post.* washingtonpost.com/business/interactive/2021/black
-executives-american-companies

p. 165   "disrespect, tiredness, and burnout." Ward, M. (2020, April 9).
DEI execs are burning out amid the billion-dollar push to
diversify corporate America. *Business Insider.* businessinsider
.com/dei-leaders-risk-burnout-diversity-equity-inclusion
-addressing-systemic-racism-2021-4

p. 166   "'being less scared to discuss race issues.'" Bersin, J. (2020,
July 20). *Chief Diversity Officer: The toughest job in business.* The
Josh Bersin Company. joshbersin.com/2020/07/chief-diversity
-officer-the-toughest-job-in-business

p. 166   "many may actively avoid these topics." Gurchiek, K. (2020,
August 3). *SHRM research finds need for more awareness,
understanding of racial inequality.* Society for Human Resource
Management. shrm.org/hr-today/news/hr-news/pages/shrm
-research-finds-need-for-more-awareness-understanding-of
-racial-inequality.aspx

Chapter 9: Meeting in the Middle

p. 171   "taxonomy of leadership behavior." Yukl, G. (2012, September 2).
Effective leadership behavior: What we know and what
questions need more attention. *Academy of Management
Perspectives*, 26(4), 66–85. doi.org/10.5465/amp.2012.0088

p. 172   "interpersonal demands of managerial roles." Beck & Harter,
Why great managers are so rare.

p. 172   "sponsor to help them succeed at work." Perez, T. (2019, July 31).
Sponsors: Valuable allies not everyone has. Payscale. payscale.com/
data/mentorship-sponsorship-benefits

p. 172 "they are the same race as their manager." Giuliano, L., Levine, D.I., & Leonard, J. (2011, January 1). Racial bias in the manager-employee relationship: An analysis of quits, dismissals, and promotions at a large retail firm. *Journal of Human Resources*, 46(1), 26–52. doi.org/10.3368/jhr.46.1.26

p. 172 "do not have the same experiences in the workplace as their White counterparts." McKinsey & Co. (2021, February). *Race in the workplace: The Black experience in the US private sector.* mckinsey.com/featured-insights/diversity-and-inclusion/race-in-the-workplace-the-black-experience-in-the-us-private-sector

p. 173 "Meisha-ann said." Martin, M. (2022, February 2). Personal communication.

p. 173 "many managers lead people who do not look like them." Wilson, V., Miller, E., & Kassa, M. (2021, June 8). *Racial representation in professional occupations.* Economic Policy Institute. epi.org/publication/racial-representation-prof-occ

p. 176 "particularly Black employees." McKinsey & Co., *Race in the workplace.*

p. 176 "(about nine hours each day) working." US Bureau of Labor Statistics. (n.d.). Average hours employed people spent working on days worked, 2019 averages. *Graphics for Economic News Releases.* www.bls.gov/charts/american-time-use/emp-by-ftpt-job-edu-h.htm

p. 176 "were quitting their jobs en masse." Cohen, A. (2021, May 10). How to quit your job in the great post-pandemic resignation boom. *Bloomberg Businessweek.* bloomberg.com/news/articles/2021-05-10/quit-your-job-how-to-resign-after-covid-pandemic

p. 176 "desire for greater flexibility and autonomy." Patton, C. (2021, July 20). *2 keys to stopping the "Great Resignation"? Flexibility and trust.* Human Resource Executive. hrexecutive.com/2-keys-to-stopping-the-great-resignation-flexibility-and-trust

p. 176 "including restaurants, healthcare, and technology." Cook, I. (2021, September 15). Who is driving the Great Resignation? *Harvard Business Review.* hbr.org/2021/09/who-is-driving-the-great-resignation; Jaffe, G. (2021, November 6). "It's a walkout!" Inside the fast-food workers' season of rebellion. *The Washington Post.* washingtonpost.com/nation/interactive/2021/rebellion-mcdonalds-bradford-pa/

p. 176 "being 'micromanaged and disrespected.'" Miller, K.L. (2021, October 7). "Micromanaged and disrespected": Top reasons

workers are quitting their jobs in "The Great Resignation."
The Washington Post. washingtonpost.com/business/2021/10/
07/top-reasons-great-resignation-workers-quitting/

p. 177 "the pandemic accelerated its pace and impact." Williamson, I.O.
(2021, November 12). The "Great Resignation" is a trend that
began before the pandemic—and bosses need to get used to it.
The Conversation. theconversation.com/the-great-resignation
-is-a-trend-that-began-before-the-pandemic-and-bosses-need
-to-get-used-to-it-170197

p. 177 "including covering monthly expenses." Mercer. (2021,
October). *The truth about what employees want: A guide to
navigating the hyper-competitive US labor market.* mercer.us/
content/dam/mercer/attachments/private/us-2021-inside
-employees-minds-report.pdf

p. 177 "'Do you *see me?*'" Gist, M. (2020). *The extraordinary power
of leader humility: Thriving organizations—great results.*
Berrett-Koehler.

p. 181 "managers support their career ambitions." Yo-Jud Cheng, J.,
& Groysberg, B. (2021, June 18). Research: What inclusive
companies have in common. *Harvard Business Review.* hbr.org/
2021/06/research-what-inclusive-companies-have-in-common;
Ely, R.J., & Thomas, D.A. (2020, November–December).
Getting serious about diversity: Enough already with the
business case. *Harvard Business Review.* hbr.org/2020/11/
getting-serious-about-diversity-enough-already-with-the
-business-case

p. 181 "for that matter!)." Yo-Jud Cheng & Groysberg, Research: What
inclusive companies have in common.

p. 181 "to be change agents, too." Mills, A.K. (2016). *Everyone is a
change agent: A guide to the change agent essentials.* Engine for
Change Press.

Chapter 10: HR and the Science of Inclusive Leadership

p. 187 "'did not like women,' as Reuters reported." Dastin, J. (2018,
October 10). *Amazon scraps secret AI recruiting tool that showed
bias against women.* Reuters. reuters.com/article/us-amazon
-com-jobs-automation-insight/amazon-scraps-secret-ai
-recruiting-tool-that-showed-bias-against-women-idUSKC
NIMK08G

p. 188   "scored higher on job performance measures." This latter
procedure was used mostly in very large organizations, like
government departments, where they could invest the needed
time and data that would allow us to set aside data for research
purposes only. This approach, though useful, is less accepted
in our fast-paced world, where decision makers want valid
data much sooner. This pressure to do things quickly is one of
the reasons why AI is so attractive to organizational decision
makers. It is also the very reason why those who use AI tools for
selection might miss the unintentional consequences of their
work, like in the Amazon example.

p. 188   "most commonly used performance criteria." Gatewood, R.,
Feild, H., & Barrick, M. (2016). *Human resource selection* (8th
ed.). Cengage Learning.

p. 189   "a variety of talent decisions." US Equal Opportunity
Employment Commission. (2007, December 1). *Employment
tests and selection procedures.* eeoc.gov/laws/guidance/
employment-tests-and-selection-procedures

p. 190   "how some of the new tools are designed." Walter C. Borman,
University of South Florida Department of Psychology Faculty:
psychology.usf.edu/faculty/wborman. Wally is a former
president of the Society for Industrial and Organizational
Psychology (SIOP) and a world-renowned researcher on
performance measurement, citizenship behavior, employee
selection, and personality assessment.

p. 190   "influences my thinking about this work." Paul Spector:
paulspector.com. Paul "wrote the book" on introductory
I/O psychology and is a world-renowned researcher on job
satisfaction and counterproductive work behavior. See Baas,
J., Boyack, K., & Ioannidis, J.P.A. (2021). *August 2021 data-
update for "Updated science-wide author databases of standardized
citation indicators"* (Mendeley Data, V3). doi.org/10.17632/
btchxktzyw.3

p. 190   "AI is used for employee selection." Smith, P. (2021, September
1). *Artificial intelligence bias needs EEOC oversight, official says.*
Bloomberg Law. news.bloomberglaw.com/privacy-and-data
-security/artificial-intelligence-bias-needs-eeoc-oversight
-official-says

p. 191   "resource for evaluating AI-based HR tools." Society for
Industrial and Organizational Psychology. (2022, January 29).

SIOP statement on the use of artificial intelligence (AI) for hiring: Guidance on the effective use of AI-based assessments. siop.org/Portals/84/docs/SIOP%20Statement%20on%20the%20Use%20of%20Artificial%20Intelligence.pdf

p. 191 "regulating the use of AI in hiring processes." Vanian, J. (2021, November 27). AI hiring software faces a regulatory reckoning. *Fortune.* fortune.com/2021/11/23/a-i-hiring-software-regulation-new-york

p. 191 "from the use of AI-powered HR tech." Business Roundtable. (2022, January 26). *Business Roundtable launches responsible AI initiative.* businessroundtable.org/business-roundtable-launches-responsible-ai-initiative

p. 194 "'focus for the foreseeable future.'" Macey, W.H., & Fink, A.A. (Eds.). (2020). *Employee surveys and sensing: Challenges and opportunities.* Oxford University Press.

p. 197 "'impede nuanced understanding of health disparities.'" Kader, F., & Lanford Smith, C. (2021). Participatory approaches to addressing missing COVID-19 race and ethnicity data. *International Journal of Environmental Research and Public Health, 18*(12), 6559. doi.org/10.3390/ijerph18126559

p. 198 "measure the outcomes from your REDI work." Williams, J.C., & Dolkas, J. (2022, March–April). Data-driven diversity. *Harvard Business Review.* hbr.org/2022/03/data-driven-diversity

p. 198 "via the EEO-1 form." US Equal Employment Opportunity Commission, *EEO-1 data collection.*

p. 198 "experience *within* their identity groups." PBS. (n.d.). *Race: The power of an illusion.* pbs.org/race/000_General/000_00-Home.htm

p. 198 "other social and economic measures." Tamir, C., Budiman, A., Noe-Bustamante, L., & Mora, L. (2021, March 25). *Facts about the US Black population.* Pew Research Center. pewresearch.org/social-trends/fact-sheet/facts-about-the-us-black-population

p. 198 "spans about fifty ethnic groups." National Alliance on Mental Illness. (n.d.). *Asian American and Pacific Islander.* nami.org/Your-Journey/Identity-and-Cultural-Dimensions/Asian-American-and-Pacific-Islander

p. 199 "more desirable than darker skin." Alter, A.L., Stern, C., Granot, Y., & Balcetis, E. (2016, December). The "bad is Black" effect: Why people believe evildoers have darker skin than do-gooders. *Personality and Social Psychology Bulletin, 42*(12), 1653–1665. doi.org/10.1177/0146167216669123

p. 199   "'prefer to solely check white.'" Hernández, T.K. (2021). Latino anti-Black bias and the Census categorization of Latinos: Race, ethnicity, or other? In J.H. Costa Vargas & M.-K. Jung (Eds.), *Antiblackness*. Duke University Press.

p. 199   "referencing a quote from Marta Cruz-Janzen." Dr. Hernández's work includes an explanation of why she uses the term "Latino" to describe a group that might be variously called Hispanic/ Latino, Latina/o, Latinx, and so on. Cruz-Janzen, M.I. (2007). Madre patria (mother country): Latino identity and rejection of Blackness. *Trotter Review*, *17*(1): 79–92. scholarworks.umb.edu/ trotter_review/vol17/iss1/6

p. 199   "a phenomenon termed 'colorism.'" Jones, T. (n.d.). *3 things you should know about global colorism*. Harvard Kennedy School. wappp.hks.harvard.edu/3-things-you-should-know-about -global-colorism

p. 202   "'irrelevant in many business circles.'" Edmondson Bell, E.L.J., & Nkomo, S.M. (2019). Race in organizations: Often cloaked but always present. In L.M. Roberts, A.J. Mayo, & D.A. Thomas (Eds.), *Race, work, and leadership: New perspectives on the Black experience*. Harvard Business Review Press.

p. 202   "'need for attention to issues of race.'" Pew Research Center. (2021, March 18). *Majorities of Americans see at least some discrimination against Black, Hispanic, and Asian people in the US*. pewresearch.org/fact-tank/2021/03/18/majorities-of -americans-see-at-least-some-discrimination-against-black -hispanic-and-asian-people-in-the-u-s

p. 202   "only 46 percent of White Americans agree." Pew Research Center. (2021, August 12). *Deep divisions in Americans' views of national racial history—and how to address it*. pewresearch.org/ politics/2021/08/12/deep-divisions-in-americans-views-of -nations-racial-history-and-how-to-address-it

p. 202   "'a distraction from our company's real work.'" Wilson, J. (2021, August 11). *Are DEI initiatives "distracting from real work"?* HR Reporter. hrreporter.com/focus-areas/diversity/ are-dei-initiatives-distracting-from-real-work/358823

p. 204   "even within the academy of psychological science." Avery, D.R. (2021, August). *What if organizational scientists really cared about race?* [Mainstage keynote]. Annual Convention of the American Psychological Association, virtual; Cascio, W.F., & Aguinis, H. (2008). Research in industrial and organizational psychology from 1963 to 2007: Changes, choices, and trends. *Journal of Applied Psychology, 93*(5), 1062–1081. doi.org/10.1037/0021 -9010.93.5.1062

p. 205   "'alleviate issues of race in the workplace.'" Mitchell, R. (2018, November 20). Learning to talk about race in the workplace. *The Harvard Gazette.* news.harvard.edu/gazette/story/2018/11/ silence-is-a-statement-brings-topic-of-race-into-the-workplace

p. 206   "your race-based REDI efforts." Coqual. (2022, February 25). *Black equity index: Tracking commitment to racial equity in the workplace.* coqual.org/wp-content/uploads/2022/02/BEI -white-paper-FINAL-02.22.pdf

p. 207   "optimize the talent of employees from diverse backgrounds." Cowley, S. (2020, February 13). Katherine W. Phillips, 47, dies: Taught the value of difference. *The New York Times.* nytimes. com/2020/02/13/business/katherine-w-phillips-dead.html

p. 209   "never on race." Kahneman, D., Rosenfield, A.M., Gandhi, L., & Blaser, T. (2016, October). Noise: How to overcome the high, hidden cost of inconsistent decision making. *Harvard Business Review.* hbr.org/2016/10/noise; Axt, J.R., & Lai, C.K. (2019). Reducing discrimination: A bias versus noise perspective. *Journal of Personality and Social Psychology, 117*(1), 26–49. doi.org/10.1037/pspa0000153

p. 209   "behavior can change attitudes." Kelly, G. (1955). *The psychology of personal constructs* (2 vols.). W.W. Norton.

p. 210   "essential for human survival." World Health Organization. (2015, June 3). *Biodiversity and health.* who.int/news-room/fact -sheets/detail/biodiversity-and-health

p. 210   "'capture the benefits of diversity?'" Cowley, Katherine W. Phillips, 47, dies.

p. 210   "Racial bias is contagious." Willard, G., Isaac, K.-J., & Carney, D.R. (2015, May). Some evidence for the nonverbal contagion of racial bias. *Organizational Behavior and Human Decision Processes, 128*, 96–107. doi.org/10.1016/j.obhdp.2015.04.002

p. 213   "'also experience a loss in motivation.'" Ward, DEI execs are burning out amid the billion-dollar push to diversify corporate America.

p. 213   "'communicating, and perpetuating, prejudicial attitudes.'" Jacoby-Senghor, D.S., Rosenblum, M., & Brown, N.D. (2021, May). Not all egalitarianism is created equal: Claims of nonprejudiced inadvertently communicate prejudice between ingroup members. *Journal of Experimental Social Psychology, 94.* doi.org/10.1016/j.jesp.2021.104104

p. 213   "'but take no real action.'" Counts, L. (2021, June 25). *Why insisting you're not racist may backfire.* BerkeleyHaas. newsroom. haas.berkeley.edu/research/why-insisting-youre-not-racist -may-backfire

p. 215   "wait longer for promotion opportunities than White employees." Coqual. (2021.) *Equity at work: Fulfilling its promise through process.* coqual.org/wp-content/uploads/2021/10/ Coqual-Equity-At-Work-Key-Findings-FINAL.pdf

p. 215   "'people of color in leadership roles.'" Colacurcio, M. (2021, December 23). Personal communication.

p. 215   "intersectional pay gaps persist." Barroso, A., & Brown, A. (2021, May 25). *Gender pay gap in US held steady in 2020.* Pew Research Center. pewresearch.org/fact-tank/2021/05/ 25/gender-pay-gap-facts; Patten, E. (2016, July 1). *Racial, gender wage gaps persist in US despite some progress.* Pew Research Center. pewresearch.org/fact-tank/2016/07/01/ racial-gender-wage-gaps-persist-in-u-s-despite-some-progress

p. 217   "avoiding those that do not?" Creary, S.J., Rothbard, N., & Scruggs, J. (2021, May). *Improving workplace culture through evidence-based diversity, equity and inclusion practices.* Wharton School, University of Pennsylvania. wharton.upenn.edu/wp -content/uploads/2021/05/Applied-Insights-Lab-Report.pdf

Chapter 11: Seeing All Women Clearly

p. 220   "'discrimination on a daily basis.'" Waterhouse, T. (2020, December 11 & 22). Personal communication.

p. 220   "underrepresentation is worse at higher levels." McKinsey & Co. & Lean In. *Women in the workplace 2021.*

p. 220   "even product design decisions." Criado Perez, C. (2019). *Invisible women: Data bias in a world designed for men.* Abrams Press.

p. 221   "detailed in the report *PowHER Redefined.*" nFormation & Billie Jean King Leadership Initiative, *PowHER Redefined.*

p. 221   "according to Deepa." Purushothaman, D. (2021, August 24). Personal communication.

p. 221   "in Dr. Kecia Thomas's research." Thomas, K.M., Johnson-Bailey, J., Phelps, R.E., Tran, N.M., & Johnson, L. (2013). Women of color at midcareer: Going from pet to threat. In L. Comas-Díaz & B. Greene (Eds.). *Psychological health of women of color: Intersections, challenges, and opportunities.* Praeger.

p. 222 "when you are 'other' than those you lead." Thomas, K.M. (2019). Leading as "the other." *Journal of Leadership & Organizational Studies, 26*(3), 402–406. doi.org/10.1177/1548051819849005

p. 222 "*The Warmth of Other Suns* and *Caste.*" Wilkerson, I. (2010). *The warmth of other suns: The epic story of America's Great Migration.* Vintage; Wilkerson, I. (2020). *Caste: The origins of our discontents.* Random House.

p. 222 "illustrates the 'invisibility' that Black women face." Wilkerson, I. (2020, July 1). America's enduring caste system. *The New York Times.*

p. 225 "more likely to be marginalized and silenced." Melaku, T.M., Beeman, A., Smith, D.G., & Johnson, W.B. (2020, November– December). Be a better ally. *Harvard Business Review.*

p. 225 "particularly women of color, in the workplace." Johnson, personal communication.

p. 225 "This is a fallacy." Thomas, D.A. (2001, April). Race matters. *Harvard Business Review.* hbr.org/2001/04/race-matters

p. 225 "both get more comfortable with each other." American Psychological Association. Mere-exposure effect. *APA Dictionary of Psychology.* dictionary.apa.org/mere-exposure-effect

p. 228 "dos and don'ts of effective allyship." Ray, S. (2020, December 15). *A different kind of diversity program is inspiring people to be better allies—and be OK with making mistakes.* Microsoft. news .microsoft.com/features/a-different-kind-of-diversity-program -is-inspiring-people-to-be-better-allies-and-be-ok-with-making -mistakes

p. 228 "Ellen said in an interview with me." Taaffe, E. (2021, March 2). Personal communication.

p. 229 "culture drives business performance." Boyce, A.S., Nieminen, L.G., Gillespie, M.A., Ryan, A.M., & Denison, D.R. (2015). Which comes first, organizational culture or performance? A longitudinal study of causal priority with automobile dealerships. *Journal of Organizational Behavior, 36*(3), 339–359. doi.org/10.1002/job.1985

Chapter 12: How to Build a Workplace Culture

p. 232 "feeling seen, connected, supported, and proud." Coqual.
(2020). *The power of belonging: What it is and why it matters in
today's workplace.* coqual.org/wp-content/uploads/2020/09/
CoqualPowerOfBelongingKeyFindings090720.pdf

p. 233 "culture as 'essential' to the business." Raymond James. (2021).
Blueprint. raymondjames.com/-/media/rj/dotcom/files/about
-us/blueprint.pdf

p. 234 "$1.18 trillion in client assets by 2021." Raymond James. (n.d.).
Raymond James quick facts. raymondjames.com/-/media/rj/
dotcom/files/our-company/investor-relations/financial
-reports/quick_facts.pdf

p. 236 "routinely outperforms the competition." Raymond James. (n.d.).
Accolades: Growing success. raymondjames.com/corporations
-and-institutions/accolades

p. 237 "Tom James and Bo Godbold." James, T.A. (2021, September 10
& 17; 2022, January 18). Personal communication; Godbold, F.
(2021, September 1). Personal communication.

p. 237 "lucrative coin and silver dealership." Young, S. (2013, January 1).
Thomas A. James, MBA, 1966. Harvard Business School Alumni.
alumni.hbs.edu/stories/Pages/story-bulletin.aspx?num=2781

p. 242 "in Tech's Clough Undergraduate Learning Commons."
Georgia Tech Institute for Diversity, Equity, and Inclusion.
(2019, August 30). *Trailblazers: The struggle and the promise.
Georgia Tech integration history meets recognition through art.*
diversity.gatech.edu/news/trailblazers-struggle-and-promise

p. 242 "continues to work on enhancing diversity." Ellingrud, K.,
Krivkovich, A., Nadeau, M.-C., & Zucker, J. (2021, October 21).
*Closing the gender and race gaps in North American financial
services.* McKinsey & Co. mckinsey.com/industries/financial
-services/our-insights/closing-the-gender-and-race-gaps-in
-north-american-financial-services

Further Reading

. . . .

Chapter 1: CEOs Can Change America, One Employee at a Time

Fee, K. (2021, March 22). *Economic inclusion 2000–2020: Labor market trends by race in the US and states.* Federal Reserve Bank of Cleveland. clevelandfed.org/en/newsroom-and-events/publications/economic-commentary/2021-economic-commentaries/ec-202106-labor-market-trends-by-race-in-the-us-and-states.aspx

US Equal Employment Opportunity Commission. (n.d.). *African-Americans in the American workforce.* eeoc.gov/special-report/african-americans-american-workforce

US Equal Employment Opportunity Commission. (n.d.). *Facts about race/color discrimination.* eeoc.gov/laws/guidance/facts-about-racecolor-discrimination

Chapter 2: Yesterday Explains Today

Hannah-Jones, N. (2021). *The 1619 project: A new origin story.* One World.

Kendi, I.X., & Blain, K.N. (Eds.). (2021). *Four hundred souls: A community history of African America, 1619–2019.* One World.

Smith, C. (2021). *How the word is passed: A reckoning with the history of slavery across America.* Little, Brown.

Chapter 3: The Diversity and Inclusion Imperative

Johansen, B. (2012). *Leaders make the future: Ten new leadership skills for an uncertain world.* Berrett-Koehler.

McGhee, H. (2021). *The sum of us: What racism costs everyone and how we can prosper together.* One World.

283

Samuelson, J. (2021). *The six new rules of business: Creating real value in a changing world.* Berrett-Koehler.

Chapter 4: Understand Your Beliefs about REDI
Daniel Tatum, B. (2017). *"Why are all the Black kids sitting together in the cafeteria?" And other conversations about race.* Basic Books.
Greer, J., & Dixon, P. (2020). *Bias, racism and the brain: How we got where we are and what needs to happen next.* OBI Press.
Morgan Roberts, L., Mayo, A., & Thomas, D.A. (2019). *Race, work, and leadership: New perspectives on the Black experience.* Harvard Business Review Press.

Chapter 5: The Truth about Working in Your Organization
Bush, M.C. (2018). *A great place to work for all: Better for business, better for people, better for the world.* Berrett-Koehler.
Livingston, R. (2021). *The conversation: How seeking and speaking the truth about racism can radically transform individuals and organizations.* Currency.
Perry, B.D., & Winfrey, O. (2021). *What happened to you? Conversations on trauma, resilience, and healing.* Flatiron Books.
Rosenberg, M.B. (2015). *Nonviolent communication: A language of life.* 3rd ed. PuddleDancer Press.

Chapter 6: CEO and Board Using the Same Playbook
Archambeau, S. (2020). *Unapologetically ambitious: Take risks, break barriers, and create success on your own terms.* Grand Central Publishing.
Bryant, A., & Sharer, K. (2021). *The CEO test: Master the challenges that make or break all leaders.* Harvard Business Review Press.
Israel, T. (2020). *Beyond your bubble: How to connect across the political divide—skills and strategies for conversations that work.* American Psychological Association.

Chapter 7: The C-Suite Inclusion Infusion
Andersen, E. (2009). *Being strategic: Plan for success; out-think your competitors; stay ahead of change.* St. Martin's Press.
Carucci, R. (2020, November 23). How to actually encourage employee accountability. *Harvard Business Review.* hbr.org/2020/11/how-to-actually-encourage-employee-accountability

Doerr, J. (2018). *Measure what matters: How Google, Bono, and the Gates Foundation rock the world with OKRs.* Portfolio.

Galbraith, J.R. (1974, May). Organization design: An information processing view. *Interfaces, 4*(3), 28–36. doi.org/10.1287/inte.4.3.28

Galbraith, J.R. (2012). The future of organization design. *Journal of Organization Design, 1*(1): 3–6. doi.org/10.7146/jod.6332

Mallick, M. (2020, September 11). Do you know why your company needs a Chief Diversity Officer? *Harvard Business Review.* hbr.org/2020/09/do-you-know-why-your-company-needs-a-chief-diversity-officer

Mills, A.K. (2021). *Change tactics: 50 ways change agents boldly escape the status quo.* Engine for Change Press.

Syndio. (2021). *2021 pay equity trends: What leaders in fair pay are doing differently.* info.synd.io/2021-pay-equity-trends-report

Chapter 8: A CDO with Resources and Political Clout

Harrell, J.A. (2021, September 8). *A new model for the DE&I business case: Moving DE&I from the P&L to the balance sheet.* Emory Business: Insights from Goizueta Business School. emorybusiness.com/2021/09/08/a-new-model-for-the-dei-business-case-moving-dei-from-the-pl-to-the-balance-sheet

Lahiri, I. (2008). *Creating a competency model for diversity and inclusion practitioners.* The Conference Board Council Perspectives. conference-board.org/pdf_free/councils/TCBCP005.pdf

Mallick, M. (2020, September 11). Do you know why your company needs a Chief Diversity Officer? *Harvard Business Review.* hbr.org/2020/09/do-you-know-why-your-company-needs-a-chief-diversity-officer

Chapter 9: Meeting in the Middle

Amaechi, J. (2021). *The promises of giants: How you can fill the leadership void.* Nicholas Brealey.

nFormation & Billie Jean King Leadership Initiative. (2021). *PowHER redefined: Women of color reimagining the world of work.* powherredefined.com

We All Count. (n.d.). *The data equity framework.* weallcount.com/the-data-process

Williams, R., & Weber, K. (2019). *Learning to lead: The journey to leading yourself, leading others, and leading an organization.* Greenleaf Book Group.

Chapter 10: HR and the Science of Inclusive Leadership

Cox, G., & Peters, K. (2021, November 2). *L&D's DEI blind spot: Perpetuating inequity?* Chief Learning Officer. chieflearningofficer.com/2021/11/02/lds-dei-blind-spot-perpetuating-inequity

International Organization for Standardization. (2021). *Human resource management: Diversity and inclusion* (ISO 30415:2021). webstore.ansi.org/Standards/ISO/ISO304152021

Manswell, A. (2015). *Listen in: Crucial conversations on race in the workplace.* JRM Publishing.

Mattingly, V., Grice, S., & Goldstein, A. (2022). *Inclusalytics: How diversity, equity, and inclusion leaders use data to drive their work.* Mattingly Solutions.

Chapter 11: Seeing All Women Clearly

Edmonson Bell, E.L.J., & Nkomo, S.M. (2001). *Our separate ways: Black and White women and the struggle for professional identity.* Harvard Business School Press.

Giddings, P. (1984). *When and where I enter: The impact of Black women on race and sex in America.* William Morrow.

Harts, M. (2019). *The memo: What women of color need to know to secure a seat at the table.* Seal Press.

Jerkins, M. (2018). *This will be my undoing: Living at the intersection of Black, female, and feminist in (White) America.* Harper Perennial.

Johnson, W.B., & Smith, D.G. (2016). *Athena rising: How and why men should mentor women.* Harvard Business Review Press.

Jones, C., & Shorter-Gooden, K. (2003). *Shifting: The double lives of Black women in America.* Harper Perennial.

Purushothaman, D. (2022). *The first, the few, the only: How women of color can redefine power in corporate America.* Harper Business.

Smith, D.G., & Johnson, W.B. (2020). *Good guys: How men can be better allies for women in the workplace.* Harvard Business Review Press.

Chapter 12: How to Build a Workplace Culture

Yo-Jud Cheng, J., & Groysberg, B. (2021, June 18). Research: What inclusive companies have in common. *Harvard Business Review.* hbr.org/2021/06/research-what-inclusive-companies-have-in-common

Index

Task Force on Climate-Related
Financial Disclosures, 65
task-oriented leadership, 171
Taylor, Breonna, 2, 34
Thomas, Kecia M., 204, 205, 207,
210, 213, 221
Thompson, Donald, 73
traditionally underrepresented
or subordinated groups, use of
term, 31
transparency, 66. *See also*
accountability
trauma, race-based, 58
Trillium, 65
Trouillot, Michel-Rolph, 35
trust, 59, 60
Tulsa Race Massacre (1921), 40–41

unconscious bias. *See* implicit
(unconscious) bias
United Kingdom: Commission
on Race and Ethnic Disparities
(CRED), 123–24
United Nations: Sustainable
Development Goals (SDGs),
59–60, 60–61

values-based leadership, 237–38
variation, use of term, 32
vision, 152–53, 155–57, 160, 168, 170
vision worksheet, 158–59
Voting Rights Act (1965), 40

Wade, Sophie, 94
Wallaert, Matt, 87
Ward, Marguerite, 165
Washington, Glynn, 200
Waterhouse, Tom, 219–20
Welch, Jack, 146
White Americans: as allies, 227;
vs. Black perceptions, 41–42, 202;
capitalization of "White," 32;
conscious bias and, 82; disparities

vs. Black Americans, 22, 41–43;
implicit (unconscious) bias, 71–72,
81–82; poor leadership and,
172–73; systemic bias and, 83
Wilkerson, Isabel, 222, 224
Williams, David, 58
Williams-Morris, Ruth, 58
Wilson, Kathlyn, 86
women: allyship and, 227–28;
discrimination against at work,
219–20; discrimination against
Black women, 22, 57–58, 132, 221,
222, 224; discrimination against
women of color, 220–21, 221–22;
executive summary, 230; making
room for perspectives of, 228–29;
questions to consider, 230; strategies for countering discrimination,
225, 227
Workhuman, 173
workplace. *See* culture; organizations

Yukl, Gary, 171–72

About the Author

. . . .

GENA COX, PhD, is an organizational psychologist, executive coach, and speaker. She coaches corporate leaders, start-up executives, and board directors to enhance their leadership impact in disrupted workplaces—and build the inclusive organizations their employees deserve.

Over a twenty-five-plus-year career, Cox has advised clients in financial services, healthcare, technology, and manufacturing, most within post-M&A, turnaround, and executive transition contexts. As a result, her clients enhanced employee experience and productivity, and ultimately enjoyed upticks in customer experience and financial outcomes.

National publications, including *Harvard Business Review*, *Fortune*, and *Fast Company*, have featured her ideas. Cox holds a PhD in industrial and organizational psychology and is a certified professional coach. She is active in leadership roles in the Society for Industrial and Organizational Psychology.

Away from work, she is a bicycling enthusiast, a museum and art lover, and cannot resist the call of a white-sand beach.

Get Gena's Curated Resources
for Inclusive Leaders

. . . .

THANK YOU! I am so honored that you have read this book. Are you ready to take your REDI work to the next level? Inclusive leadership requires an Inclusion MBA (Mindset, Boldness, Action), so I have curated additional resources at **leadinginclusion.com** to help you progress on your Inclusion MBA journey, including these:

- **Thinking tools:** workbooks, conversation scripts, research summaries, and other curated content.

- **Information about bulk purchases,** so you can share this book with your colleagues and friends.

- **Customized help,** including booking me to speak at your event, deliver a keynote speech, or participate in a panel discussion. I also love the fireside chat format, making it easy to have honest conversations that address what's top of mind. And you can also figure out if I would be the ideal executive coach for you or another leader you know.

- **The REDI community,** through which you'll receive periodic curated content to help you continue your inclusive workplace journey, one employee at a time.

Go to leadinginclusion.com